Religion and Life

Revision Guide

SECOND EDITION

VICTOR W. WATTON

Hodder Murray

A MEMBER OF THE HODDER HEADLINE GROUP

The Publishers would like to thank the following for permission to reproduce copyright material:

Photo credits
p.25 © Images.com/CORBIS

Text acknowledgements
Exam questions courtesy of Edexcel Limited. Edexcel Ltd, accepts no responsibility whatsoever for the accuracy or method of working in the answers given.

Every effort has been made to trace all copyright holders, but if any have been inadvertently overlooked the Publishers will be pleased to make the necessary arrangements at the first opportunity.

Hodder Headline's policy is to use papers that are natural, renewable and recyclable products and made from wood grown in sustainable forests. The logging and manufacturing processes are expected to conform to the environmental regulations of the country of origin.

Orders: please contact Bookpoint Ltd, 130 Milton Park, Abingdon, Oxon OX14 4SB. Telephone: (44) 01235 827720. Fax: (44) 01235 400454. Lines are open 9.00–6.00, Monday to Saturday, with a 24-hour message answering service. Visit our website at www.hoddereducation.co.uk

© Victor W. Watton
First published in 2006 by
Hodder Murray, an imprint of Hodder Education,
a member of the Hodder Headline Group
338 Euston Road
London NW1 3BH

Impression number   10 9 8 7 6 5 4 3 2 1
Year   2010 2009 2008 2007 2006

Artwork by Adrian Barclay (Beehive Illustrations)
Cover photo Corbis & Photodisk
Typeset in Baskerville and Gill Sans by Dorchester Typesetting Group Limited
Printed in Great Britain by Hobbs the Printers Ltd, Totton, Hants.

A catalogue record for this title is available from the British Library

ISBN-10: 0 340 92684 8
ISBN-13: 978 0340 926 840

CONTENTS

Introduction
How to use this guide
Exam techniques

introduction

HOW TO USE THIS GUIDE

The aim of this guide is to help you revise and improve your exam skills so that you attain your highest possible performance in GCSE Religious Studies.

You should read the section on exam techniques first so that you know what types of questions are asked by Edexcel and what sorts of answers are expected. You should then work through sections 1–4. If you are not doing coursework, you should then work through either option 1 or option 2 of section 5 (whichever option you have been taught).

Sections 1–4 are sections of the specification on which you will have to answer questions in the exam. Each section is divided into topics which you should use in the following way:

1 Learn the key words for the topic.
2 Learn the key facts for the topic.
3 Learn the main facts for the topic.

Each section ends with some practice questions. Try these and check your answers against the full mark answers at the end of the book to see how well you have done.

If your answers show that you are having problems:

- check whether your problem is that you cannot remember the facts. If it is, relearn the appropriate chapter.
- check whether your problem is that you have not answered the question properly. If it is, re-read the exam techniques section.

EXAM TECHNIQUES

TECHNIQUES FOR CHOOSING QUESTIONS

The exam paper is divided into five sections if you are not doing coursework, and four sections if you are doing coursework.

In each section you will have a choice of two questions:

Section 1: question 1 or 2
Section 2: question 3 or 4
Section 3: question 5 or 6
Section 4: question 7 or 8
Section 5: question 9 or 10

All the questions have part (a) for 2 marks, part (b) for 6 marks, part (c) for 8 marks and part (d) for 4 marks.

Go through both questions in a section, ticking the parts of the question you think you can get a good mark on, for example:
1 tick for (a), 3 ticks for (b), 4 ticks for (c), and 2 ticks for (d).

Add up the ticks you have given for each question and choose the question that has the most ticks.

Remember! You have to choose a complete question – this means you must answer parts (a), (b), (c) and (d) from the same question.

TYPES OF QUESTIONS IN SECTIONS 1–4

PART (A) QUESTIONS

These are short-answer knowledge questions, for example, 'What is cohabitation?'. You do not need to write full sentences for your answers. These questions often ask for the meanings of the key words.

PART (B) QUESTIONS

These are knowledge questions, which require a one or two paragraph answer. They will usually begin with the words **outline** or **describe**:

- **Outline** means you write one or two sentences about a number of issues. For example, 'Outline THREE types of religious experience' means write one or two sentences on the numinous, on miracles, on conversion or on answered prayer.
- **Describe** means to write in depth about one particular issue. For example, 'Describe one religious experience' means write one or two paragraphs on one particular experience someone has had.

If you are asked to outline or describe different attitudes, it means you must write about at least two attitudes.

PART (C) QUESTIONS

These are all understanding questions and usually begin with the word **explain**.

You must go through the question and highlight the key words that tell you how to write your answer:

- **Why** means you must use the word 'because' and give reasons. For example, 'Explain why some Christians are against divorce' means you must answer in a way such as, 'Some Christians are against divorce because they believe that the marriage vows are between the couple and God as well as each other ...' (then go on and give any more reasons you can think of).

- **How** means you must connect two ideas. For example, 'Explain how the teachings of one religion other than Christianity could help to promote racial harmony' means you must write out one teaching and explain how it could lead followers of the religion to help racial harmony, then write out another teaching and how it too could lead followers to help racial harmony and continue in this way.

- **Explain why there are different attitudes** means you must identify one attitude and explain why people believe it, then identify another attitude and explain why people believe that. For example, 'Explain why there are different attitudes to the role of women in Christianity' means give reasons why some Christians think women cannot be priests or lead worship, then give reasons why some Christians think women can be priests and leaders.

PART (D) QUESTIONS

These are evaluation questions. They begin with a statement in quotation marks and then ask:

'Do you agree? Give reasons for your opinion, showing that you have considered another point of view.'

Even though the question asks 'Do you agree?', it is not enough just to give your opinion. You must:

- look at a view that is different from your opinion and say, with reasons, why people have this view
- state why you disagree with this view using evidence from your knowledge of Religious Studies

- come to a conclusion restating whether you agree with the statement or not with a brief reason.

It is very important that you use religious examples from the course and that you show you have thought about the statement before coming to a conclusion.

EXAMPLE OF A GOOD EVALUATION ANSWER

'Having a religious wedding ceremony makes no difference to how the marriage works out.'

Do you agree? Give reasons for your opinion, showing you have considered another point of view. In your answer, you should refer to the teachings of at least one religion.

a The view you disagree with, and your reasons

Many people think that having a religious wedding ceremony makes no difference to how the marriage works out. Such people claim that the figures show marriages that began with a religious ceremony are just as likely to end in divorce as registry office weddings.

b Why you disagree with this view

However, it seems to me that this view ignores a lot of the evidence and so I disagree with the statement in the question. In a Christian wedding ceremony, the bride and groom have to make promises to each other in the sight of God. They have to promise to love and cherish each other, in sickness and in health, until death parts them. Because they have made these promises to God as well as to each other, they have an extra reason for keeping them. Also a Christian wedding ceremony involves a sermon and Bible readings about the nature of marriage and how to make it work and prayers asking for God's help to make the marriage work.

c Conclusion – restating your opinion

So, it seems to me that religious wedding ceremonies do help to make a marriage work. At the end of the day, a long religious ceremony with promises made to God in front of all your family and friends is bound to have an effect on your marriage.

TYPES OF QUESTIONS IN SECTION 5

If you are not doing coursework, you will also have to answer one question from section 5. **You should only answer the question on the topic you have studied.**

This section is marked out of 23, i.e. 3 marks more than the other questions. Each question is divided into three parts: part (a) for 4 marks, part (b) for 8 marks and part (c) for 8 marks.

You should spend at least 30 minutes on the question and it is a good idea to do this question first so that you do not run out of time.

Part (a) is a knowledge question, the same as the other part (b) questions.

Part (b) is an understanding question, the same as the other part (c) questions, but you should write a longer answer.

Part (c) is an evaluation question, the same as the other part (d) questions, but marks are out of 8 rather than 4 and should have a longer answer.

The extra 3 marks are for your Quality of Written Communication, so make sure you:
• write in sentences
• use paragraphs
• do not use bullet points or numbering
• take care with your spelling.

SECTION

1

Believing in God

1.1 Religious upbringing

MAIN FACTS

If someone is brought up by religious Christian parents, they will believe in God from the beginning of their life:

- they will be baptised
- they will be taken to worship God with their parents
- they will be taught to pray to God every day
- they will be expected to thank God and remember God's good gifts at various religious festivals especially at Christmas and Easter
- they will go to Sunday school and learn about God
- they are likely to go to a school, maybe a church school, where nearly everyone believes in God and so they are expected to believe in God.

With an upbringing like this, it is natural to believe in God, and such people may never even think that God might not exist.

KEY FACTS

Having a religious upbringing leads to belief in God because children are taught that God exists and they spend most of their time with people who believe God exists.

Remember

You only need to learn one religion for this section. This guide only gives information on Christianity for section 1. If you are a Muslim, Jew, Hindu, or Sikh, you can answer on your own religion. The questions will simply say 'Choose one religion'.

KEY WORDS

Conversion when your life/religion is changed.

Miracle an event that seems to break a law of science and the only explanation for which seems to be God.

Numinous the feeling of the presence of something greater than you.

Prayer an attempt to contact God, usually through words.

Remember

If you are asked to describe a religious experience, you need to write about one particular experience only, e.g. a miracle or an answered prayer.

MAIN FACTS

Religious experience means the ways in which people come into direct contact with God. There are various types of religious experience:

- It can be just a feeling you get when you are in a holy building, say your prayers, or even look up at the stars and feel in the presence of something greater than yourself. This is called the numinous.
- It can be a more definite feeling of God's presence which makes you much more religious and changes your life (e.g. St Paul on the road to Damascus). This is called a conversion experience.
- It can be experiencing a miracle, e.g. when Jesus brought Jairus' daughter back to life, it seemed to break laws of science and only be explained by the existence of God.
- It can be having a prayer answered, e.g. someone prays for God to help them out of a problem and the problem disappears.

Any of these experiences are almost certain to lead the person who experiences them to believe in God.

KEY FACTS

People claim to experience God in miracles, answered prayers, the numinous and conversion. Religious experience makes people feel that God is real.

1.3 Design and belief in God

MAIN FACTS

If things work together following a plan to bring something about, we say they are designed. The universe seems to be designed because of:

- the way the universe works according to scientific laws such as gravity
- the way humans grow from a tiny blueprint of DNA
- the way complex mechanisms work, such as the eye allowing people to see
- the way the Big Bang worked with the laws of science to produce a universe of order.

This leads people to believe in God because:

- if something is designed, it must have a designer
- the universe is designed
- the only possible designer of the universe is God
- therefore, people believe, God must exist.

KEY FACTS

The universe seems to be designed, and people think that means God must exist because a design needs a designer.

KEY WORD

Design when things are connected and seem to have a purpose: for example, the eye is designed for seeing.

1.4 Causation and belief in God

MAIN FACTS

Causation is the idea that if something happens, something must have caused it to happen. This idea can lead people to believe in God because:

- if we look at things in the world, we see they have a cause
- anything caused to exist must be caused by something else
- therefore the universe itself must have a cause
- only God could be the cause of the universe
- therefore, God must exist.

KEY FACTS

The way everything seems to have a cause makes people think that the universe must have a cause, which must be God.

KEY WORD

Causation the idea that everything has been caused (started off) by something else.

1.5 The search for meaning and purpose

MAIN FACTS

Many people cannot believe that human beings are here by chance. They think that life must have a meaning and purpose. There must be a reason for our lives. When they search for a meaning and purpose in life, they find it is given by God. They follow a religion which tells them how to live so that when they die, they will be rewarded by eternity in heaven. If only God and life after death can give life meaning and purpose, they believe this proves that God must exist.

KEY FACTS

Some people believe in God because they believe there must be a reason for humans being here and only God can give our lives meaning and purpose.

Remember

'Meaning and purpose' means why are we here? And what should we be trying to do with our lives?

1.6 Religion and belief in God

MAIN FACTS

- 86 per cent of the world's population belong to a religion. It seems hard to believe that all those people are wrong, and this leads some people to believe God must exist.
- The fact that most religions seem to share a lot of similar beliefs about God, life after death, the need to pray and worship, etc. makes many people believe that there must be a force that religions are trying to contact and that force could only be God.

KEY FACTS

Some people believe that because so many people believe in God and religion, God must exist.

Does it make something true if lots of people believe it? Think of how many people used to believe the earth was flat.

1.7 Non-religious explanations of the world and agnosticism and atheism

MAIN FACTS

Scientific explanations of the world can lead people to become agnostics (not sure whether God exists) or atheists (believing that God does not exist).

- Science now explains how the Universe and the Earth came into being through the Big Bang.
- Science now explains how humans came into being through evolution.
- If science can explain where humans and the world came from without needing God, people may doubt the arguments for God's existence and begin to think that God does not exist.

KEY FACTS

Some people think that if the creation of the Universe, the Earth and people can be explained away by science, it is unlikely that God exists.

KEY WORDS

Agnosticism not being sure whether or not God exists.

Atheism believing that God does not exist.

Remember

Many atheists think that if God could use a miracle to feed 5000 people with five loaves and two fishes, then he could use miracles to feed all the starving.

1.8   Non-religious explanations of miracles

MAIN FACTS

Many people believe in God because of miracles that are supposed to have happened, like Jesus coming back from the dead. But science can explain many miracles. There is also the problem that you have to rely on witnesses to believe a miracle and they might be telling lies. Some people argue that if God existed he would not send a miracle to save a few people, and allow thousands to starve to death. The fact that God does not save people from earthquakes, tsunamis, etc. makes some people think he does not exist.

KEY FACTS

There are lots of problems with believing in miracles, such as people telling lies about miracles and the idea that a good God would perform miracles to help more people. Also, science can explain many miracles.

1.9 Unanswered prayers

MAIN FACTS

Religious people are supposed to pray and some people feel the presence of God when they pray. But if people pray and do not feel God's presence, they may begin to feel he does not exist. Unanswered prayers can lead people to become agnostics or atheists. God is supposed to care for those who worship him, but if people pray and pray, and God never answers their prayers, that person may well become agnostic or atheist.

KEY FACTS

If people never feel God's presence when they pray, or if their prayers are never answered, they may begin to feel that there is no God.

1.10 Evil and suffering

MAIN FACTS

Evil and suffering in the world lead some people to become agnostics or atheists. Moral evils like wars and muggings can be blamed on humans. But people suffer from the effects of such things as disease, starvation and earthquakes. These natural evils must be the fault of God – indeed they are often called acts of God. If God is good (benevolent), he must want to get rid of such things. If God is all-powerful (omnipotent), he must be able to get rid of such things. The fact that these things continue to exist leads some people to believe that there is no God.

KEY FACTS

Some people do not believe in God because they think that there would be no evil and suffering in a world created by a good, powerful God.

KEY WORDS

Moral evil actions done by humans that cause suffering.

Natural evil things that cause suffering, but have nothing to do with humans, for example, earthquakes.

1.11 The problem of evil and suffering

MAIN FACTS

Christians and people who believe in God find the existence of evil and suffering a problem because:

- they believe that God is good (benevolent), but if God is good he ought not to want evil and suffering in his world
- they believe that God has the power to do anything (omnipotent) but if God is all-powerful, he must be able to get rid of evil and suffering from the world he created
- however, there is evil and suffering in the world, so either God is not good or God is not all-powerful, or God does not exist.

KEY FACTS

People who believe in God find evil and suffering a problem because God should not want such things to happen and he also ought to be able to get rid of them, but he does not.

KEY WORDS

Benevolent the belief that God is all-good/loving.

Omnipotent the belief that God is all-powerful.

Omniscient the belief that God knows all that has happened and that will happen.

1.12 How Christians respond to the problem of evil and suffering

MAIN FACTS

- Many Christians respond to the problem of evil and suffering by believing that God knows the answer, but that people cannot. Jesus showed people that God wants them to fight against evil and suffering, so people should follow the example of Jesus and pray for those who suffer and give them practical help wherever possible.
- Some Christians think that God could not give humans free will unless they had the chance to do evil things (being free is part of being made in God's image). Humans have used their free will to do evil things and this has brought suffering into the world. So evil and suffering is the fault of humans not God.
- Other Christians believe that this life is a sort of test in which people prepare their souls for heaven. If there were no evil and suffering, they would not be able to develop as good people, because being good involves helping those who suffer and fighting against evil. If people follow the Christian way, their souls will become good and God will send them to heaven when they die.
- All Christians believe they must respond to suffering by trying to help those who suffer either by praying for them or by working for Christian Aid, becoming a nurse, etc.

KEY FACTS

Christians respond to the problem of evil and suffering by:
- praying for those who suffer
- helping those who suffer
- claiming that evil and suffering are the fault of humans misusing their free will
- claiming that evil and suffering are part of a test to prepare people for heaven.

Remember
You can write about the Muslim, Jewish, Hindu or Sikh responses to evil and suffering if you would rather.

Remember
'Respond to' means how they explain it **and** what they do to stop it.

PRACTICE QUESTIONS ✓

a What is a miracle? (2 marks)
b Describe a religious experience. (6 marks)
c Choose ONE religion and explain how its followers respond to the problem of evil and suffering. (8 marks)
d 'No one can be sure that God exists.'
Do you agree? Give reasons for your opinion, showing you have considered another point of view. (4 marks)

SECTION 2

Matters of Life and Death

2.1 Christian attitudes to life after death

MAIN FACTS

All Christians believe that this life is not all there is. There are two Christian beliefs about what happens after death.

1. Resurrection of the body

Many Evangelical Protestants and other Christians believe that when people die they stay in the grave until the end of the world when God will raise everyone's body and judge them. True Christians will go to heaven and everyone else will go to hell. They believe in resurrection of the body because:

- it is what St Paul teaches in 1 Corinthians 15
- Jesus' body rose from the dead
- it is part of the Christian creeds.

2. Immortality of the soul

Many Christians do not believe in the resurrection of the body. They believe in immortality – that the soul, or mind, is immortal and lives on after death. When people die their souls go straight to heaven. They believe this because:

- Jesus said the criminal on the cross would be in paradise straight after death
- the communion of saints teaches that living and dead Christians can communicate with each other
- things like near-death experiences (the soul leaves the body and goes down a tunnel of light to God) show the immortality of the soul.

Christian beliefs about life after death may differ, but all Christians believe in it and this gives their lives purpose and meaning.

KEY FACTS

- Some Christians believe in resurrection – that when they die they will stay in the grave and be raised on the Last Day.
- Some Christians believe in immortality of the soul – that when the body dies, the soul lives on in heaven.

KEY WORDS

Immortality the idea that the soul lives on after the death of the body.

Resurrection the belief that, after death, the body stays in the grave until the end of the world, when it is raised.

2.2 Reasons for Christian attitudes to life after death

MAIN FACTS

There are many different attitudes to life after death. Apart from the main difference about resurrection of the body or immortality of the soul, Christians also differ about who will go to heaven and whether there is a hell.

There are many reasons for these differences:

- The Bible says different things about heaven, hell, resurrection and immortality.
- Many Christians find it hard to believe that an all-loving God will send people to hell for ever.
- Living in a multi-faith society makes it hard to believe that good Muslims, Hindus, Sikhs and Jews will be sent to hell.
- More evidence about the paranormal makes it easier to believe in immortality of the soul.

KEY FACTS

As well as having different ideas about resurrection and immortality, Christians have different attitudes about whether there is a hell and whether only Christians will go to heaven.

!

Remember

If only Christians go to heaven, then very good religious people like Gandhi and the Dalai Lama will go to hell.

2.3 Why Christians believe in life after death

MAIN FACTS

All Christians believe that there is life after death because:
- Jesus rose from the dead
- the Bible says that there is life after death
- Churches teach that there is life after death
- the creeds say that there is life after death
- there is evidence of life after death from such things as near-death experiences and the paranormal
- they believe that life after death gives life meaning and purpose.

KEY FACTS

All Christians believe in life after death because they believe Jesus rose from the dead, and it is part of the teachings of Jesus and the Church.

!

Remember

The creeds are statements of Christian belief that all Christians should agree with.

Islam and life after death

MAIN FACTS

Muslims believe in the resurrection of the body. They believe that when people die, they stay in the grave until the Last Day when God will bring the world to an end. Then everyone will be raised with resurrected bodies for a final judgement. God will judge people on whether they have been good or bad Muslims; the good will go to heaven for ever, the bad will go to hell for ever.

This belief makes Muslims aware that everything they do is known to God and will be used by God to decide whether to send them to heaven or hell. Therefore their behaviour is affected by their beliefs about life after death.

Why Muslims believe in life after death

All Muslims believe in life after death because:

- it is what the Qur'an teaches and the Qur'an is the word of God
- they believe that life is a test from God, which only makes sense if there is life after death. Belief in life after death gives their lives meaning and purpose
- it is taught in the hadith of the Prophet.

Some Muslims also believe in life after death because of the evidence of the paranormal.

KEY FACTS

Muslims believe in life after death because it is taught in the Qur'an and the hadith of the Prophet. They believe that the body stays in the grave until the Last Day when it will be raised, judged by God and sent to either heaven or hell.

Muslims try to do what God wants because if they do not, they will be sent to hell on the Last Day.

Attention

You only need to answer on one religion other than Christianity, so only revise the religion you have been taught.

Remember

Hadith are records of what it is thought Muhammad said and did.

Judaism and life after death

MAIN FACTS

Judaism teaches that this life is a preparation for a future life with God. Some Jews believe in the resurrection of the body, others believe in an immortal soul.

Jews are not sure what life after death will be like, but the fact that they call cemeteries 'The House of Life' shows they believe that God will look after them after death. Many Jews believe that if they confess their sins before they die, they will be forgiven and God will let them live with him in everlasting happiness.

These beliefs help Jews to understand that life has purpose and meaning. Their aim is to serve God by following the mitzvot and so have eternal bliss.

Why Jews believe in life after death

Jews believe in life after death because:
- it is the teaching of the Tenakh
- it is the teaching of the Talmud
- it is one of the Thirteen Principles of the Jewish faith
- belief in life after death gives life meaning and purpose
- they cannot believe that God would allow death to be the end.

Some Jews also believe in life after death because of the evidence for the paranormal.

KEY FACTS

Jews believe in life after death because it is taught in the Tenakh and Talmud. Jews are not sure what life after death will be like, but they believe good Jews will be in bliss.

!

Remember

The Thirteen Principles are a summary of Jewish beliefs accepted by all Orthodox Jews.

Hinduism and life after death

MAIN FACTS

Hindus believe that all humans have immortal souls which are continually reborn until they achieve release (moksha) and become one with the Divine (Brahman). Hindus have many different views on how moksha is to be achieved:

- Some believe it is achieved by following one's dharma in the four ashramas.
- Others through dedication to Krishna or a guru.
- Others through meditation practices like yoga.

Most Hindus would follow a mixture of these (and perhaps others) as their way of achieving moksha.

Why Hindus believe in life after death

Hindus believe in life after death because:

- it is the teaching of the Bhagavad Gita, the Upanishads and the Vedas
- it is the teaching of all the Gurus and swamis
- reincarnation makes sense of life.

Many Hindus believe in the evidence of the paranormal for the existence of souls and reincarnation.

KEY FACTS

All Hindus believe in life after death because it is taught in the Hindu holy books and by the Gurus and swamis. Hindus believe that the soul is reborn after death until it is pure enough to gain release and unity with Brahman.

Remember

'Moksha' means release from the cycle of death and rebirth.

Sikhism and life after death

MAIN FACTS

Sikhism teaches that all humans have an immortal soul (divine spark), which is reborn into another body after death. This process (samsara) carries on until the soul is pure enough to achieve release (mukti).

The way to mukti is by changing from being human-centred (manmukh) to being God-centred (gurmukh) by following the teaching of the Gurus.

After mukti, the soul enters eternal bliss, often called heaven – a beautiful place which is the home of God.

There are some different interpretations of this teaching among Sikhs:

- Some Sikhs are not aware of the belief in reincarnation because they are taught that following the Sikh way leads to heaven when they die.
- Some believe only good Sikhs will go to heaven.
- Some believe all good people will go to heaven whatever their religion.

Sikhs believe this life is a preparation for heaven.

Why Sikhs believe in life after death

Sikhs believe in life after death because:

- it is the teaching of the Guru Granth Sahib, the living Guru
- all ten human Gurus believed in life after death
- reincarnation makes sense of life, making sure the good are rewarded and the evil punished, and giving everyone a second chance.

Many Sikhs believe in the evidence of the paranormal for reincarnation.

KEY FACTS

Sikhs believe that everyone has a soul which is reborn unless a person becomes God-centred when the soul is released (mukti) and goes to heaven. Sikhs believe in life after death because:

- it is taught in the Guru Granth Sahib
- it was the teaching of the Gurus
- it gives their lives meaning and purpose.

(!)

Remember

Reincarnation is the belief that souls are born into another body after death.

2.5 Non-religious reasons for believing in life after death

2.6 Why some people do not believe in life after death

MAIN FACTS

Some people do not believe in life after death because:
- the main evidence for life after death is in holy books which contradict each other. For example, the Qur'an teaches resurrection, the Bhagavad Gita teaches reincarnation, some of the Bible teaches immortality of the soul
- no one has undoubtedly returned from the dead
- science shows that when the body dies, the brain dies, and life-support machines show that the brain dies, so what could survive death?
- there is no place where life after death could take place.

KEY FACTS

Some people do not believe in life after death because the only evidence is in holy books which contradict each other. They do not see where life after death could take place.

Remember

Holy books are books which a religion claims to be the words of God. The Bible is the holy book of Christianity, the Qur'an is the holy book of Islam.

2.7 The nature of abortion

MAIN FACTS

The law in the United Kingdom says that abortion is only allowed if two doctors agree that:
- the mother's life is at risk
- the mother's physical or mental health is at risk
- the child is very likely to be born severely handicapped
- there would be a serious effect on other children in the family.

Abortions cannot be carried out after 24 weeks of pregnancy.

People who argue about abortion often argue about when life begins:
- Some say it begins as soon as an egg is fertilised.
- Others say it begins when it receives a soul.
- Others say life only begins when the foetus can survive outside the womb.

KEY FACTS

Abortion is allowed in the United Kingdom if two doctors agree that there is medical reason for it. Arguments about abortion are based on when life begins.

KEY WORD

Abortion the removal of a foetus from the womb before it can survive.

2.8 Christian attitudes to abortion

MAIN FACTS

There are two different Christian attitudes to abortion.

1. Roman Catholics and many Evangelical Protestants believe abortion is always wrong because:

- there are Christian teachings on the sanctity of life
- God has created life in the mother and to prevent that life being born is murder and against God's will
- they believe that life begins at conception and, as God banned murder in the sixth commandment, all abortions should be banned.

2. Other Protestants (e.g. the Church of England) disagree with abortion, but think that in certain circumstances it is necessary to choose the lesser of two evils and so abortion must be allowed. Although they would prefer there to be no abortion, they realise that there would be too much suffering if abortion were banned. They have these views because:

- they do not believe that life begins at conception
- they believe Jesus' command to love your neighbour is the most important command
- they believe it is the duty of Christians to remove suffering
- they believe that when faced with a choice between two evils, Christians should choose the lesser evil.

KEY FACTS

Christians have different attitudes to abortion:
- Some Christians believe that abortion is always wrong because it is murder and against God's will.
- Some Christians believe that abortion is wrong, but must be allowed in some circumstances as the lesser of two evils.

KEY WORD

Sanctity of life the belief that life is sacred and belongs to God.

Remember

'The lesser of two evils' means when you are faced with a choice where whatever you choose will be wrong, but one choice will be less wrong.

Islam and abortion

MAIN FACTS

There are three different Muslim attitudes to abortion:

1. Some Muslims believe abortion should not be allowed because:
   - they believe in the sanctity of life
   - they believe life can only be given and taken by God
   - God says in the Qur'an that people should never kill their children.

2. Most Muslims believe that abortion can be allowed only if the mother's life is at risk. They believe this because:
   - the death of the unborn child is a lesser evil than the death of the mother
   - the Shari'ah says that the mother's life must always take priority.

3. Some Muslims only allow abortions up to 120 days into pregnancy for reasons such as the health of the mother or problems with the baby's health. They believe this because:
   - the hadith and decisions of Muslim lawyers state that abortion is not allowed after 120 days of pregnancy because that is when the foetus becomes a child.

KEY FACTS

- Some Muslims think that abortion should never be allowed.
- Some Muslims think that abortion can only be allowed if the mother's life is in danger.
- Some Muslims think that abortion is allowed until 120 days into pregnancy because this is when the foetus becomes a child.

Attention

You only need to answer on one religion other than Christianity, so only revise the religion you have been taught.

Remember

The Shari'ah is the holy law of Islam.

Judaism and abortion

MAIN FACTS

There are two different Jewish teachings on abortion.

1. Some Jews believe that abortion is always wrong because:
   - many passages from the Tenakh say that death and life are in the hands of God and so life is sacred; it is something only God can give and take
   - life begins at conception and the sixth commandment forbids taking life, so abortion is wrong.

2. Other Jews believe that abortion can be allowed if the mother's life is in danger, or there are problems with the baby's health. They believe this because:
   - there are statements in the Torah that say a woman is allowed an abortion if the pregnancy threatens her life
   - some rabbis teach that as life does not begin until the foetus is able to survive outside the mother's body, abortions are allowable.

KEY FACTS

- Some Jews believe abortion is always wrong because life is in God's hands.
- Some Jews believe abortion can be allowed in certain circumstances because it is taught in the Torah.

Remember
The Tenakh is the holy book of Judaism and has the same books as the Christian Old Testament.

Remember
The Torah is the first five books of the Tenakh containing God's laws given to Moses.

Hinduism and abortion

MAIN FACTS

There are at least three different attitudes to abortion among Hindus.

1. Some Hindus teach that there should be no abortion. They believe this because of the belief in ahimsa (non-violence) and the teachings of many swamis and gurus.

2. Some Hindus teach that abortion should be allowed only if the mother's life is in danger. They believe this because the teaching on ahimsa means that violence should not be done to the mother by the foetus.

3. Some Hindus teach that abortion is allowable under any circumstances. They believe this because the Bhagavad Gita says that it is impossible to kill the soul, as the soul of the foetus will just be put into another body.

Abortion is available on demand in India where a large number of Hindus live.

KEY FACTS

- Some Hindus think abortion should never be allowed.
- Some Hindus think abortion can only be allowed if the mother's life is in danger.
- Some Hindus think abortion is allowed in any circumstances.

Remember

The Bhagavad Gita is a Hindu holy book containing guidance from Lord Krishna.

Sikhism and abortion

MAIN FACTS

There are different attitudes to abortion in Sikhism.

1. Some Sikhs believe that abortion is wrong and should only be used if the mother's life is in danger or she has been raped. They believe this because:
   - they believe life is sacred and begins at conception
   - they believe in the lesser of two evils and the death of the foetus is less evil than the death of the mother.

2. Some Sikhs allow abortion according to UK law. They believe this because:
   - each individual is part of God's essence so they believe the mother is more important than the foetus as she is an individual, but the foetus is not
   - they believe sanctity of life involves the lives of the mother and other family members as well as the life of the foetus.

For these reasons they allow abortion if it involves the removal of suffering.

KEY FACTS

- Many Sikhs believe abortion is wrong except for when the mother's life is at risk or she has been raped.
- Some Sikhs believe in the UK law on abortion because they believe sanctity of life is connected to removing suffering.

Remember

UK law on abortion is that an abortion is allowed if two doctors agree that the life of the mother is at risk, or the health of the mother, the foetus or existing children are at risk.

KEY WORDS

Assisted suicide providing a seriously ill person with the means to commit suicide.

Euthanasia an easy and gentle death.

Non-voluntary euthanasia ending someone's life painlessly when they are unable to ask, but when there is good reason for thinking they would want death, for example, switching off a life-support machine.

Voluntary euthanasia the situation where someone dying in pain asks another person to end his/her life painlessly.

MAIN FACTS

- Changes in medical skills and technology mean that euthanasia is now discussed more.
- Life-support machines, new medical technology to keep handicapped babies alive, and better drugs to fight cancer all mean that people are being kept alive by medicine – often in agony.
- The law says nothing can be done by doctors that could be thought of as euthanasia. However, recent decisions by the courts have allowed doctors to switch off life-support machines and stop feeding patients who are in a persistent vegetative state.

KEY FACTS

There are various types of euthanasia which are all aimed at giving an easy death to those suffering intolerably. It is more of a problem now because medicine is more likely to keep people alive for longer.

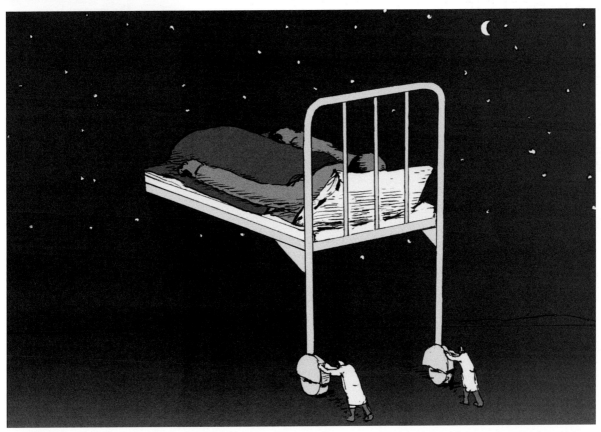

If a doctor's job is to save lives, should doctors be asked to kill patients with low quality of life? Who decides who is to live and who is to die?

2.11 Christian attitudes to euthanasia

MAIN FACTS

All Christians oppose the practice of euthanasia because:

- they believe that life is sacred and should only be taken by God
- the Bible says quite clearly that Christians must not murder (sixth commandment)
- there are many statements in the Bible which say that life and death decisions belong only to God
- many Church leaders have said that life is sacred and comes from God, therefore only God can decide when someone should die
- Christians believe that doctors are required to save lives, not kill, and to allow them to kill people would be giving them double standards to follow.

However, there are some different attitudes:

- Most Christians (including Roman Catholics) accept that doctors should be allowed to give lots of pain-killing drugs even if they know it is shortening the patient's life. They also believe that expensive treatments need not be carried out to lengthen the lives of dying patients.
- Some Christians do not agree with switching off life-support machines, but many Christians believe this must be allowed when there are no signs of life.

KEY FACTS

All Christians are against euthanasia because they believe life is sacred and belongs to God. However, there are some different attitudes among Christians about switching off life-support machines.

Remember

'Quality of life' means being able to think, communicate with others, feed yourself, be free from severe pain, etc. Some people think that low or no quality of life is a reason for euthanasia.

Islam and euthanasia

MAIN FACTS

Islam does not allow euthanasia because:

- the Qur'an bans suicide and declares that no soul can die without God's permission
- Muhammad said that a Muslim soldier who committed suicide because he was dying a painful death on the battlefield would not be allowed into heaven
- Muslims believe life is a test from God and so if people use euthanasia, they are cheating in the test by trying to speed it up.

However, there are different attitudes to switching off life-support machines:

- Some Muslims think switching off a life-support machine is the same as euthanasia and so they do not allow it.
- Some Muslims allow life-support machines to be switched off because, recently, Muslim lawyers have agreed that life-support machines can be switched off when there are no signs of life.

KEY FACTS

All Muslims are against euthanasia because they believe life is sacred and belongs to God. However, there are some different attitudes among Muslims about switching off life-support machines.

Attention

You only need to answer on one religion other than Christianity, so only revise the religion you have been taught.

Remember

Muslims believe the length of a person's life is set by God to give them the right number of tests. Shortening life by euthanasia would be cheating in the test.

Judaism and euthanasia

MAIN FACTS

1. Most Jews do not allow euthanasia because:

   - many passages from the Tenakh say that death and life are in the hands of God
   - the Authorised Daily Prayer Book services say that life belongs to God and only he can decide when someone is to die.

2. Some rabbis allow euthanasia in the sense of switching off life-support machines and not 'striving officiously to keep alive' so that the soul is free to go to God. They believe this because they think that striving to keep someone alive is interfering with God's will.

KEY FACTS

All Jews are against euthanasia because they believe life is sacred and belongs to God. However, there are some different attitudes among Jews about switching off life-support machines.

Remember

'Striving officiously to keep alive' means such things as giving expensive, distressing treatments to a patient to extend their life by a few days.

Hinduism and euthanasia

MAIN FACTS

There are two different attitudes to euthanasia among Hindus:

1. Some Hindus teach that euthanasia is permissible as long as it is the wish of the dying person. They believe this because it is the immortal soul, and not the body, which is part of God, therefore the soul cannot be harmed. All that is being done is aiding the soul to gain release.

2. Other Hindus teach that euthanasia is wrong because they believe that all life is sacred as every soul is actually or potentially a part of God. The teaching of ahimsa means that euthanasia is unacceptable because it must involve inflicting violence on the patient.

KEY FACTS

- Some Hindus agree with euthanasia if the dying person wants to die easily because it releases the soul.
- Other Hindus only allow life-support machines to be switched off and no other form of euthanasia because life is sacred.

Remember

'Immortal soul' means the part of a person that is supposed to live on after death.

Sikhism and euthanasia

MAIN FACTS

1. Most Sikhs are against all forms of euthanasia because:
   - Sikh teaching on violence to humans means that euthanasia would bring bad karma and prevent mukti
   - life is a gift from God which should not be taken by humans
   - the law of karma says only God can take life at the right time.

2. Some Sikhs believe that euthanasia is wrong, but life-support machines can be switched off and doctors do not need to strive to keep alive because:
   - if someone is brain-dead their life has already ended, so it is not being taken
   - striving to keep alive is preventing the soul from moving on, so it is stopping the law of karma
   - release of the soul is the aim of Sikh life, so people should not be kept alive artificially.

KEY FACTS

- Most Sikhs are against euthanasia because they believe life and death should be in the hands of God, and that killing brings bad karma and so will prevent mukti.
- Some Sikhs accept not striving to keep alive and switching off life-support machines because not to do so would prevent the release of the soul.

Remember

Karma are actions which have an effect on the purity of the soul.

PRACTICE QUESTIONS ✓

a What is euthanasia? (2 marks)

b Choose ONE religion, other than Christianity, and outline its teachings about euthanasia. (6 marks)

c Explain why there are different beliefs among Christians about life after death. (8 marks)

d 'Religious people should never have abortions.'
Do you agree? Give reasons for your opinion, showing you have considered another point of view. In your answer, you should refer to at least one religion. (4 marks)

Marriage and the Family

3.1 Changing attitudes to cohabitation and marriage

MAIN FACTS

Attitudes to sex and marriage have changed greatly.
Fifty years ago:

- sex before marriage and cohabitation were regarded as sins
- people were expected to marry in church before they were 25
- most households had a husband, wife and children.

Today:

- most people have sex before they are married
- cohabitation is accepted and most couples live together before marriage
- most households are not headed by a married couple
- the average age for marriage has increased greatly
- only about 35 per cent of marriages take place in church.

These changing attitudes have affected sexual health. In 2003, more than ten per cent of the population had had a sexually transmitted infection.

KEY FACTS

Fifty years ago, most people only had sex in marriage, and they married in church. Today, most people have sex before they marry, fewer people marry, cohabiting is acceptable and only a minority of marriages take place in church.

KEY WORDS

Cohabitation living together without being married.

Marriage a man and woman legally joined so that they are allowed to live together and, usually, have children.

KEY WORDS

Pre-marital sex sex before marriage.

Promiscuity having sex with a number of partners without wanting a relationship with them.

Adultery having sex with someone other than your marriage partner (also called extra-marital sex).

Remember

Questions on sex outside marriage mean you have to write about sex before marriage and adultery.

MAIN FACTS

Most Christians believe that sex should only happen in marriage.

Pre-marital sex

Most Christians believe sex before marriage is wrong because:

- God gave sex for people to have children so it should only happen between married couples so that children are born into a family
- the Bible teaches that fornication (sex before marriage) is wrong
- all the Churches say that sex before marriage is a sin.

Some Christians believe sex before marriage is all right as long as the couple love each other, are in a long-term relationship and intend to marry eventually. They believe this because:

- Jesus taught that love is the most important thing
- the Church has to come to terms with modern life.

Extra-marital sex

All Christians believe that adultery is wrong because:

- it breaks the wedding vows
- it breaks one of the Ten Commandments.

KEY FACTS

All Christians believe adultery is wrong, as it breaks one of the Ten Commandments.

- Most Christians believe that sex before marriage is wrong because the Bible teaches this.
- Some Christians believe that sex before marriage can be accepted with certain conditions.

Islam and sex outside marriage

Attention

You only need to answer on one religion other than Christianity, so only revise the religion you have been taught.

Remember

Muslims follow the example of Muhammad because they believe he was 'the perfect exemplar'.

MAIN FACTS

Islam condemns all sex outside marriage.

Pre-marital sex

Islam does not allow sex before marriage and boys and girls are kept apart after they reach puberty. This is because:
- sex before marriage is condemned in the Qur'an
- the Qur'an says that girls and boys should be separated after puberty
- God gave sex for people to have children so it should only happen between married couples so that children are born into a family.

Extra-marital sex

All Muslims believe that adultery is wrong because:
- it is condemned by God in the Qur'an
- it breaks the marriage contract
- Islam says the family is very important, and adultery would damage it.

KEY FACTS

Muslims believe that sex before marriage and adultery are wrong because the Qur'an teaches this.

Judaism and sex outside marriage

MAIN FACTS

Judaism is against all sex outside marriage.

Pre-marital sex

Most Jews are against sex before marriage and some Orthodox Jews keep boys and girls apart after they reach puberty. This is because:

- sex before marriage is condemned in the Torah
- the Talmud says that sex should only happen in marriage
- God gave sex for people to have children so it should only happen between married couples so children are born into a family.

Some Jews believe sex before marriage is all right as long as the couple love each other, are in a long-term relationship and intend to marry eventually. They believe this because:

- they think Judaism has to come to terms with modern life.

Extra-marital sex

All Jews believe that adultery is wrong because:

- it is condemned by God in the Torah
- it breaks the marriage contract
- Judaism says the family is very important, and adultery would damage it.

KEY FACTS

All Jews believe adultery is wrong as it breaks one of the Ten Commandments.

- Most Jews believe that sex before marriage is wrong because the Torah teaches this.
- Some Jews believe that sex before marriage can be accepted with certain conditions.

Remember

The Talmud is a collection of writings about Jewish laws and morals.

Hinduism and sex outside marriage

MAIN FACTS

Hinduism is against all sex outside marriage.

Pre-marital sex

Sex before marriage is not allowed because:

- sex is not allowed in the student stage of life
- the Hindu scriptures say that sex should only happen in marriage
- sex is to have children, so it should only happen between married couples so that children are born into a family.

Extra-marital sex

All Hindus believe that adultery is wrong because:

- it is breaking one's duty and so will stop one gaining moksha
- it betrays the marriage partner
- Hinduism says the family is very important, and adultery would damage it.

KEY FACTS

Hindus believe that sex before marriage and adultery are wrong. Sex is only allowed in the householder stage of life.

!

Remember

An ashrama is a stage of life and Hinduism restricts sex to the householder stage which is called grihastha.

Sikhism and sex outside marriage

MAIN FACTS

Sikhism is against all sex outside marriage.

Pre-marital sex

Sex before marriage is not allowed because:
- all the Gurus only had sex within marriage
- the **Rahit Maryada** says that sex should only happen in marriage
- marriages are usually arranged by families so there should be no sex before the arrangement.

Extra-marital sex

All Sikhs believe that adultery is wrong because:
- it breaks the marriage union
- it is forbidden by the Rahit Maryada
- it goes against the examples of the Gurus.

KEY FACTS

Sikhs believe that sex outside marriage is wrong.
Sex before marriage is banned by the Rahit Maryada.
Adultery breaks the sacred marriage union.

!

Remember
The Rahit Maryada is a collection of rules on how Sikhs should live.

3.4 The purposes of marriage in Christianity

MAIN FACTS

Christians regard marriage as a gift from God, but they do not have to marry. The reasons (purposes) for Christian marriage are:

- for a couple to be able to live together in love till death parts them
- for a couple to have comfort and companionship whatever happens
- for a couple to be faithful to each other
- for a couple to create a Christian family.

The main features of a Christian marriage service

- The priest welcoming the couple and outlining the purposes of Christian marriage.
- Exchange of vows (promises) before God and witnesses.
- Exchange of rings showing the marriage will not end.
- Bible readings and talk on the duties of marriage.
- Prayers for God's blessing on the couple and the help of the Holy Spirit to make the marriage work.

KEY FACTS

Christian marriage is for a life-long, loving relationship and to bring up a Christian family.

These purposes can be seen in the marriage service (life-long vows, Bible readings on love and Christian families).

Remember

Being faithful means not having relationships with anyone other than your marriage partner.

The purposes of marriage in Islam

MAIN FACTS

All Muslims are expected to marry because the Prophet Muhammad was married. The reasons (purposes) for Muslim marriage are:

- to share a life of love
- to enjoy sex as God intended
- to have children and bring them up as good Muslims
- to follow the example of the Prophet Muhammad.

The main features of a Muslim marriage ceremony

There are many different types of Muslim wedding but there is usually:

- a statement in front of witnesses that both parties freely agree to marry
- signing the marriage contract which includes all financial arrangements
- readings from the Qur'an and a sermon about marriage by an imam
- prayers, by an imam, for the future of the marriage.

KEY FACTS

All Muslims should marry because Muhammad married. Muslim marriage is to share love and bring up a Muslim family. A Muslim marriage ceremony is a contract and usually includes prayers and readings from the Qur'an.

! Attention

You only need to answer on one religion other than Christianity, so only revise the religion you have been taught.

! Remember

An imam is the prayer leader of a mosque who is often the leader of the local Muslim community.

The purposes of marriage in Judaism

MAIN FACTS

All Jews are expected to marry and have children because the Torah says so.

The reasons (purposes) for marriage are:

- to share love and companionship
- to enjoy sex in the way God wants
- to have children so that the faith will not die out
- to obey God's commands in the Torah (mitzvot).

The main features of a Jewish marriage service

- The huppah (canopy) as a symbol of the new home and the couple's unity.
- The ring as a sign of dedicating themselves to each other and God.
- The marriage contract (ketubah) being signed.
- The seven blessings which link marriage to God.
- Blessing and drinking wine and smashing the wine glass.
- A wedding feast.

KEY FACTS

The purpose of Jewish marriage is to share love and companionship and continue the Jewish race by bringing up a Jewish family. These purposes can be seen in the marriage ceremony (the ketubah, the seven blessings on love and families).

!

Remember

Mitzvot are the laws in the Torah which all Orthodox Jews must follow.

The purposes of marriage in Hinduism

MAIN FACTS

All Hindus are expected to marry because it is one of the stages of life (ashramas) a Hindu must pass through. The purposes for marriage are:

- to fulfil a Hindu's role as a householder, and so gain moksha
- to enjoy sex in the way of dharma
- to find love and companionship
- to have the joy of children and bring up a Hindu family.

The main features of a Hindu marriage service

There are many different types of service, but the main features are likely to be:

- the couple taking seven steps round the sacred fire
- offerings to the gods
- prayers and hymns about the joys of marriage
- a black and gold necklace placed around wife's neck as a sign of family unity.

KEY FACTS

The purposes of Hindu marriage are to share love and companionship and complete the householder role by bringing up a Hindu family. These purposes can be seen in the marriage ceremony (seven steps showing love and sharing, prayers about the family).

Remember

Dharma is the religious duty of a Hindu.

The purposes of marriage in Sikhism

MAIN FACTS

Sikhs are expected to marry, but do not have to. The reasons (purposes) for marriage are:

- to unite a man and woman with each other and God
- to have children
- to bring up a Sikh family so the Sikh community grows
- to unite two families.

The main features of a Sikh marriage service

- The couple stand in front of the Guru Granth Sahib.
- Prayers and a reading from the Guru Granth Sahib on the duties of husbands and wives.
- The couple agree to their responsibilities.
- The lavan (wedding hymn) is sung while the bride and groom circle the Guru Granth Sahib.
- Gifts are exchanged and there is a special langar.

KEY FACTS

The purposes of Sikh marriage are to share love and companionship and follow the Gurus' examples by bringing up a Sikh family. These purposes can be seen in the marriage ceremony (the lavan showing union with God and each other).

Remember

Langar is a shared religious meal served in a special part of the gurdwara.

MAIN FACTS

It used to be difficult to divorce and divorced people were looked down on. Divorced people could not remarry in church.

Today, divorce is accepted and no one looks down on divorced people. There are lots of divorces, and as many as two in five marriages will end in divorce.

The probable reasons for these changing attitudes are:

- it is easier and cheaper to divorce
- people live longer, so they spend a longer time together (the average marriage lasted ten years a hundred years ago – just about the same as it does now)
- women are less prepared to put up with bad treatment from their husbands than they used to be
- women do not depend on their husbands for money, so they can afford to divorce.

KEY FACTS

Fifty years ago there were few divorces, people were looked down on if they divorced and remarriage was rare. Today divorce is accepted, two in five marriages end in divorce and remarriage is normal. The changes may have been caused by cheaper divorce and women having more equality.

KEY WORDS

Faithfulness staying with your marriage partner and only having sex with them.

Remarriage marrying again after being divorced.

Remember

Couples can separate without getting divorced. A divorce is a legal declaration that a couple are no longer married and are free to remarry.

MAIN FACTS

There are two different attitudes to divorce in Christianity.

1. Some Christians, especially Catholics, believe there can be no divorce because marriage is a sacrament in which the couple promise to stay together until death. Catholics do allow annulments if it can be shown that the marriage never really existed, but there can be no divorce. Catholics who have civil divorces are not allowed to remarry.

2. Most Protestant and Orthodox Christians disapprove of divorce, but believe that if a marriage goes wrong and there is no chance of bringing the couple back together, then divorce can be permitted. These Christians allow remarriage of divorced people after a talk with the minister/priest about how they will make sure the marriage works this time.

Reasons for the different attitudes

Christians have different attitudes because they interpret the Bible differently and disagree about whether marriage is a sacrament.

The Catholic Church does not allow divorce because:
- Jesus banned divorce
- when people marry, they make a covenant with God which cannot be broken without God's consent, therefore a couple can never be divorced according to God's law.

Non-Catholic Christians allow divorce because:
- God is always prepared to forgive sins if people are determined to live a new life
- in St Matthew's Gospel Jesus allows divorce for adultery.

KEY FACTS

- Roman Catholics do not allow divorce because they believe the marriage vows cannot be broken.
- Other Christians disapprove of divorce, but allow it if the marriage has broken down because Christianity teaches forgiveness.

Remember

An annulment is a declaration that a marriage never existed.

Remember

A sacrament is a special ritual, which makes an outward sign of a spiritual inner blessing.

Muslim attitudes to divorce

MAIN FACTS

Islam allows divorce, but Muslims have different attitudes to divorce.

1. **Some Muslims** think marriage is for life and divorce should not happen.
2. **Most Muslims** allow divorce, but believe there has to be a period of three months (iddah) when a couple try to restore their marriage. If this fails, they are divorced and can remarry.

Reasons for the different attitudes

There are different attitudes because of different interpretations of hadith.

Some Muslims disagree with divorce because:

- there is a hadith in which Muhammad said he hated divorce
- divorce causes family problems when marriages are arranged.

Most Muslims agree with divorce because:

- marriage is a contract in Islam, so it can be ended
- the Qur'an allows divorce and sets out regulations about it.

KEY FACTS

There are different attitudes to divorce in Islam:

- Most Muslims allow divorce because marriage is a contract.
- Some Muslims do not allow divorce because of what Muhammad said.

Attention

You only need to answer on one religion other than Christianity, so only revise the religion you have been taught.

Jewish attitudes to divorce

MAIN FACTS

Judaism allows divorce because marriage is a contract, but it is not recommended. This leads to different attitudes to divorce.

1. **Orthodox Jews** believe men should be responsible for organising divorce, but have arguments about whether a husband can refuse, if a wife wants a divorce.

2. **Reform Jews** give equal rights to men and women in divorce.

Reasons for the different attitudes

Orthodox Jews do not allow women equal divorce rights because:
- the Torah says men must give the divorce
- the halakah says that only men can apply for a divorce.

Reform Jews give equal rights because:
- they believe the Torah and halakah need bringing up to date
- they believe men and women should have equal rights in religion.

KEY FACTS

Judaism allows divorce because marriage is a contract. However, there are different attitudes to divorce.
- Orthodox Jews give special rights to men in divorce because of the Torah.
- Reform Jews give equal divorce rights to women because they think the Torah should be brought up to date.

Remember

Orthodox Jews believe the Torah is the word of God and all the mitzvot must be followed.
Reform Jews believe the Torah and the mitzvot should be adapted to modern life.

Hindu attitudes to divorce

MAIN FACTS

All Hindus expect marriage to be for life. However, there are different attitudes to divorce.

1. **Traditional Hindus** only allow divorce on grounds of cruelty or lack of children after fifteen years of marriage.

2. **Other Hindus** allow divorce if a marriage is clearly not working.

Reasons for the different attitudes

Traditional Hindus only allow divorce in very special circumstances because:

* the Law of Manu allows divorce in special circumstances
* children are an important part of the householder stage, so if a couple are childless then divorce should be allowed
* Hindu teachings on ahimsa mean that cruelty should not be accepted.

Other Hindus have easier divorce rules because:

* they think the Law of Manu is out of date
* they think arguing and quarrelling in a marriage will give bad karma.

KEY FACTS

* Some Hindus do not allow divorce because they believe marriage is for life.
* Many Hindus allow divorce especially if the couple cannot have children.

Remember

All Hindus have to go through the householder stage of life to attain moksha and part of this stage is having children.

Sikh attitudes to divorce

MAIN FACTS

All Sikhs expect marriage to be for life. However, there are different attitudes to divorce.

1. **Most Sikhs** believe there should be no divorce.

2. **Some Sikhs** think divorce should be allowed if the marriage has failed.

Reasons for the different attitudes

Most Sikhs are against divorce because:

- the Gurus did not divorce
- the Rahit Maryada says divorce is wrong
- as most marriages are arranged, divorce causes family problems.

Other Sikhs have easier divorce rules because:

- they think arguing and quarrelling in a marriage will give bad karma
- they think all Sikhs should have children, so divorce should be allowed if a couple are childless.

KEY FACTS

- Some Sikhs believe there should be no divorce because marriage is for life and the Gurus did not divorce.
- Other Sikhs allow divorce because living in hatred will bring bad karma and prevent mukti.

Remember

'The Gurus' means the ten human Gurus from Guru Nanak to Guru Gobind Singh.

MAIN FACTS

Family life has changed in the UK as attitudes to sex before marriage, cohabitation and divorce have changed.

In the 1960s:

- husband, wife and children living together (the nuclear family) was the norm.

Today:

- there are many single-parent families in which the mother is the only parent (often because of divorce)
- in many families the mother and father are not married
- as more people divorce and remarry there are more reconstituted families (twenty per cent of men over 30 are stepfathers)
- as more women go out to work, more grandparents are involved in looking after the family.

KEY FACTS

Family life has changed so that, although most children are still brought up by a mother and a father, the parents may not be married or they may have been married more than once.

Family life is the basis of society, but modern society has different types of families, any of which can bring up children.

KEY WORDS

Nuclear family mother, father and children living as a unit.

Extended family children, parents and grandparents/aunts/uncles living as a unit or very near to each other.

Re-constituted family where two sets of children (stepbrothers and sisters) become one family when their divorced parents marry each other.

3.10 Christian teachings on family life

MAIN FACTS

All Christians believe that children should be brought up in a family with a mother and father (unless one of them has died). The New Testament and the Christian Church teach that:

- parents should love their children and provide them with food, clothes, etc.
- parents should set their children a good, Christian example and encourage their children to go to church and be baptised and confirmed
- children should obey and respect their parents
- children should look after their parents if they can no longer look after themselves.

Christians believe that the family is important because:

- the Bible has many references to the importance of family life
- Christian marriage services refer to founding a family and bringing children up in a Christian environment as major purposes of marriage
- Christians believe that the family was created by God to keep society together
- Christians see the family as the basis of society.

KEY FACTS

Christianity teaches that the family is important because it is the basis of society, and a main purpose of marriage.

- Christian parents should look after their children and bring them up as Christians.
- Christian children should respect their parents and look after them when they are old.

!

Remember

The New Testament is the second part of the Bible, which records the life of Jesus and the founding of the Christian Church.

Islamic teachings on family life

MAIN FACTS

Family life is at the centre of Islam. There are many teachings about family life in the Qur'an and hadith:

- Parents have a duty to look after their children.
- Both parents have a duty to make sure their children learn all about Islam and become good Muslims.
- Children must respect their parents.
- When the parents become old, it is the duty of the children to repay their parents' kindness by looking after them.

The family is important in Islam because:

- it was created by God to keep society together
- it is the way God wants children to be brought up
- it is the place where children learn about Islam
- the Qur'an says that children are a gift from God and that parents will be judged on how well they have brought up their children
- Muhammad married and had a family, and Muslims must follow his example.

KEY FACTS

Family life is important in Islam because the family is the basis of society and Muhammad raised a family.

- Muslim parents should look after their children and bring them up as Muslims.
- Children should respect their parents and look after them when they are old.

!

Attention

You only need to answer on one religion other than Christianity, so only revise the religion you have been taught.

Jewish teachings on family life

MAIN FACTS

Jews believe that the family is at the heart of religion. The teachings on family life come from the halakah which says that:

- parents should care for their children's material needs
- parents should teach their children about Judaism and their duties as Jews
- parents should set a good example of the Jewish life especially by keeping kosher, observing Shabbat and the festivals in the home
- children are expected to respect their parents (fifth commandment) and be a comfort to them in their old age.

Jews believe that family life is very important because:

- it was created by God to keep the family together
- it is the only way God wants children to be brought up
- it is the place where children learn about Judaism and where Shabbat and the festivals are celebrated
- the family is the only way of keeping Judaism alive
- having a family is one of the mitzvot which all Jews have to follow.

KEY FACTS

Family life is important in Judaism because the family is the basis of society and the Torah says all Jews should marry and raise a family.

- Jewish parents should look after their children and bring them up as Jews.
- Children should respect their parents and look after them when they are old.

Remember

The halakah is the Jewish way of life set out in the laws of the Torah.

Hindu teachings on family life

MAIN FACTS

Family life is a central part of Hindu life. The Law of Manu, the marriage service and the statements of gurus and swamis show that:

- parents are expected to look after their children well
- parents should bring their children up in the Hindu faith
- parents should set a good example of the Hindu life and perform daily puja in the home
- children should obey and respect their parents
- children should care for their parents when they can no longer care for themselves.

The family is important in Hinduism because:

- the family was created by God to keep society together
- being a householder and bringing up a family is one of the stages of life that Hindus must go through to gain moksha
- there are many teachings about family life in the Hindu holy books
- a large part of Hindu worship (e.g. the daily puja) takes place in the home.

KEY FACTS

Family life is important in Hinduism because the family is the basis of society and Hindus are expected to raise a family as part of the householder stage of life.

- Hindu parents should look after their children and bring them up as Hindus.
- Children should respect their parents and look after them when they are old.

Remember

The Law of Manu is an ancient holy book with instructions on how Hindus should live.

Sikh teachings on family life

MAIN FACTS

Sikhism teaches that children should be brought up in a family with a mother and father. The main Sikh teachings on family life are:

- Parents are expected to look after their children well.
- Parents should bring their children up in the Sikh faith.
- Parents should set a good example of the Sikh life and perform daily prayers in the home.
- Children should obey and respect their parents.
- Children should care for their parents when they can no longer care for themselves.

The family is important in Sikhism because:

- it was created by God to keep society together
- Sikhism teaches that God is present in the home
- the family is where children learn the difference between right and wrong
- the family is where children learn about Sikhism and become Sikhs, therefore the family is the main way of keeping Sikhism alive.

KEY FACTS

Sikh parents should look after their children and bring them up as good Sikhs. Children should respect their parents and look after them in their old age. The family is important because it is the basis of society and the main purpose of marriage.

Remember

Most Sikhs teach their children about Sikhism by taking them to the gurdwara.

3.12 How Churches help with the upbringing of children

MAIN FACTS

- Church schools provide Christian education and worship as well as the normal education.
- Most Churches have infant baptism where parents dedicate their children to God and make promises about bringing their children up in a loving Christian home.
- Most churches run Sunday schools and provide classes for confirmation which teach children about right and wrong.
- Churches welcome families and have monthly family services and special services at Christmas and Easter to bring families together.
- Many churches run uniformed organisations (Cubs, Brownies, Girls' and Boys' Brigades, etc.) and youth clubs and youth activities to keep children away from immoral activities.
- Ministers/vicars/priests also act as marriage and family counsellors.
- Some Churches run marriage and family guidance services, and children's charities.

KEY FACTS

Churches help with the upbringing of children by:
- giving religious teachings at Sunday schools and providing Christian schools so the children learn about right and wrong
- providing clubs, groups, etc. to give children a moral social life
- providing help and advice on family problems for parents.

Remember
Counsellors are people who help individuals, couples or families who are having problems.

Islam and the upbringing of children

MAIN FACTS

The main way Islam helps with the upbringing of children is through the Mosque.

- Mosques run special schools (madrasahs) during evenings and weekends to educate children in Islam and teach them to read the Qur'an.
- Mosques also act as social centres with boys' and girls' clubs.
- Mosques have a family committee which helps Muslim families with problems and distributes the zakah money to families in need.
- Many mosques also help with the running of Muslim schools.

KEY FACTS

Islam helps with the upbringing of children by:

- giving religious teachings at madrasahs and providing Muslim schools so the children learn about right and wrong
- providing clubs, groups, etc. to give children a moral social life
- providing help and advice on family problems for parents.

Attention

You only need to answer on one religion other than Christianity, so only revise the religion you have been taught.

Remember

A madrasah is a mosque school for children.

Judaism and the upbringing of children

MAIN FACTS

The main way Judaism helps with the upbringing of children is through the synagogue.

- Synagogues give religious teaching about right and wrong.
- Many synagogues provide youth clubs to give a moral social life.
- Most synagogues run social centres and have a family agency committee to help keep families together.
- Many synagogues also help with the running of Jewish schools, which teach the National Curriculum in a Jewish environment.
- Many rabbis help with marriage or family problems.

KEY FACTS

Judaism helps with the upbringing of children by:
- giving religious teachings about right and wrong
- providing clubs, groups, etc. to give children a moral social life
- providing help and advice on family problems for parents.

Remember

A heder is a synagogue school.

Hinduism and the upbringing of children

MAIN FACTS

The main way Hinduism helps with the upbringing of children is through the mandir.

- Mandirs give religious teaching about right and wrong.
- Parents are expected to bring their children to mandir for worship and social gatherings.
- Many mandirs have family advice centres to help with marriage or family problems.
- Some temples also assist in the running of Hindu day schools, which teach the National Curriculum in a Hindu environment.

KEY FACTS

Hinduism helps with the upbringing of children by:
- giving religious teachings at the mandir and providing Hindu schools so the children learn about right and wrong
- providing clubs, groups, etc. to give children a moral social life
- providing help and advice on family problems for parents.

Remember

A mandir is a Hindu temple.

Sikhism and the upbringing of children

MAIN FACTS

The main way Sikhism helps with the upbringing of children is through the gurdwara.

- Most Sikh gurdwaras run evening classes or Sunday schools to teach children the basics of Sikhism.
- Parents are expected to bring their children to the gurdwara for worship and social gatherings.
- Many gurdwaras provide social activities for young Sikhs to give them a moral social life.
- Many gurdwaras have family advice centres to help with marriage or family problems.
- Some gurdwaras also assist in the running of Sikh day schools.

KEY FACTS

Sikhism helps with the upbringing of children by:
- giving religious teachings at gurdwaras and providing Sikh schools so the children learn about right and wrong
- providing clubs, groups, etc. to give children a moral social life
- providing help and advice on family problems for parents.

(!)

Remember

A gurdwara is a Sikh place of worship and social centre.

PRACTICE QUESTIONS ✓

a What is **cohabitation**? (2 marks)

b Choose ONE religion, other than Christianity, and outline the purposes of marriage in that religion. (6 marks)

c Explain why there are different attitudes among Christians to divorce. (8 marks)

d 'Living together is better than getting married.'
Do you agree? Give reasons for your opinion, showing you have considered another point of view. In your answer, you should refer to at least one religion. (4 marks)

SECTION
4

Social Harmony

4.1 The growth of equal rights for women in the UK

MAIN FACTS

A hundred years ago women did not have many rights in the United Kingdom, but during the twentieth century women gained:

- the right to vote
- the right to equal pay
- the right to act against discrimination.

These changes have also altered the roles of men and women. In 1994, almost as many women as men were in paid jobs (but more of the women's jobs were part-time).

It is now accepted that men and women have equal rights and should both have the chance of a career. This also means that men and women have to share equally in running the home and bringing up the children.

KEY FACTS

Men and women now have equal rights in the United Kingdom. During the twentieth century women gained the right to vote and to have equal pay with men.

Men and women are expected to share in the running of the home.

KEY WORDS

Equality the state of everyone having equal rights regardless of gender/race/class.

Sexism discriminating against people because of their gender (being male or female).

4.2 Christian attitudes to the roles of men and women

MAIN FACTS

There are three different attitudes to the roles of men and women in Christianity.

1. The traditional Protestant attitude

This teaches that men should be the head of the family and women should not speak in church or be ministers or priests. The reasons for this view are:

- St Paul's statements in the Bible about women not being allowed to speak in church, and having to submit to their husbands
- in Genesis 2 Adam was created first and Eve sinned first.

2. The liberal Protestant attitude

This teaches that men and women should have equal roles in life, including religion. Many Protestant Churches (e.g. Church of England, Methodist, United Reformed Church) not only have equal roles for men and women, but also have women ministers and priests. They believe this because:

- St Paul said 'There is neither ... male nor female for you are all one person in Christ'
- Jesus treated women as his equals and had women followers like Martha and her sister Mary
- they believe that Jesus chose men as his apostles because of the culture of the time and not for any religious reason.

3. The Catholic attitude

This teaches that men and women should have equal roles and equal rights because men and women have equal status in the eyes of God. However, the Catholic Church teaches that only men can become priests. They believe this because:

- Jesus only chose men to be his successors
- Jesus was a man and the priest represents Jesus in the Mass.

KEY FACTS

- Traditional Christians believe men are more important than women because this is what the Bible teaches.
- Liberal Christians believe men and women have equal roles and accept women priests.
- Roman Catholics believe men and women are equal, but only men can become priests.

(!)

Remember

Most Protestant Churches call people who are ordained 'ministers'; the Catholic Church, the Orthodox Churches and the Church of England call them 'priests'.

Islam and the roles of men and women

MAIN FACTS

There are two different attitudes to the roles of men and women in Islam.

1. The traditional attitude

This teaches that God has given men and women different roles in life. Men should support the family, while women have children and bring them up. Both men and women have the role of bringing up children as good Muslims, but men have more responsibilities because of their role as provider. Men and women should pray separately and only men have a duty to pray in the mosque. They believe this because:

• the Qur'an teaches these roles

• these are the roles shown in the Shari'ah.

2. The modern attitude

This teaches that men and women should have equal roles and that women can have a career, and should worship in the mosque. However, they believe that family commitments come first for women and that men and women should worship separately in the mosque. They believe this because:

• the Qur'an teaches that men and women are equal in religion and education

• modern society needs educated and career women.

KEY FACTS

• Traditional Muslims believe men and women have different roles and men are superior because the Qur'an teaches this.

• Modern Muslims believe men and women have equal roles, but family commitments should come first for women.

Attention

You only need to answer on one religion other than Christianity, so only revise the religion you have been taught.

Remember

Men and women worship separately in the mosque to avoid distractions.

Judaism and the roles of men and women

MAIN FACTS

There are three different attitudes to the roles of men and women in Judaism.

1. The traditional attitude

Most Orthodox Jews teach that men and women have different roles. Men should fulfil all the mitzvot, while the women only keep the mitzvot connected with the home.

They believe this because it is the teaching of the Torah and the Talmud.

2. The modern attitude

Some Orthodox Jews teach that men and women should have equal roles except in synagogue worship. They believe this because:

- the Torah says men and women are equal (Genesis 1:27)
- the mitzvot do not prevent women from having a career.

3. The liberal attitude

Reform and Progressive Jews teach completely equal roles for men and women. Men and women worship together and there are women rabbis. They believe this because:

- they believe that the Torah is not the unalterable word of God
- they interpret the Torah in the light of changes in society.

KEY FACTS

- Traditional Orthodox Jews believe that men and women have different roles in life and religion.
- Modern Orthodox Jews believe that men and women are equal but have different roles in religion.
- Reform Jews believe that men and women are completely equal and accept women as rabbis.

Remember

Bat Mitzvah is the coming of age ceremony for girls in Reform Judaism.

Hinduism and the roles of men and women

MAIN FACTS

There are three attitudes to the roles of men and women in Hinduism.

1. The traditional attitude

Traditional Hindus teach that women should be homemakers and bring up children while the men earn money and protect the family. They believe this because:

- it is what the Law of Manu teaches
- it is what is shown in the examples of the Epics.

2. The attitude of groups such as Hare Krishna

These groups teach that men and women should have completely equal roles in life and religion. They believe this because:

- they think that all souls are actually or potentially a part of the divine and so are equal.

3. The attitude of groups such as Swaminarayan

These groups give women equal status and the right to follow a career, but think they should have separate roles in the temple. They believe this because:

- they think that all souls are actually or potentially a part of the divine and so are equal
- they think that the Law of Manu and the Epics refer only to roles in the temple.

KEY FACTS

- Traditional Hindus teach that men and women have different roles.
- Some Hindus believe that men and women are completely equal.
- Some Hindus believe men and women should have equal roles in life, but different roles in the temple.

!

Remember
The Epics are the Ramayana and similar such scriptures which tell the great stories of what happened when the gods came to Earth.

Sikhism and the roles of men and women

MAIN FACTS

The religious attitude

Sikhism teaches that men and women should be completely equal, and most Sikhs believe this. Many gurdwara committees have women members and there are women religious leaders in Sikhism.

Sikhs have this attitude because:

- Guru Nanak taught that men and women are equal
- all the other Gurus taught equality and some had women helpers
- the Guru Granth Sahib teaches that God is not male or female.

The cultural attitude

Some Sikhs believe that women should be homemakers and bring up children; men should provide for the family and be religious leaders.

They have this attitude because:

- they come from the Punjab where women do not have equal rights
- they do not read the scriptures and take more notice of culture than religion.

KEY FACTS

- Some Sikhs believe that men and women are totally equal and should have the same roles in life and religion because this is the teaching of the Gurus.
- Some Sikhs are more affected by cultural attitudes and think women should be subordinate to men and not have a role in religion.

!

Remember

Guru Nanak was the first of the human Gurus and is often regarded as the founder of Sikhism.

4.4 The United Kingdom as a multi-ethnic society

> ### MAIN FACTS
>
> Britain has always been a multi-ethnic society, being a mixture of Celts, Romans, Angles, Saxons, Danes, Jutes, Vikings and Normans. It has also had a history of giving asylum to those suffering persecution, for example French Protestants in the seventeenth century and Russian Jews in the nineteenth century.
>
> During the nineteenth century, the United Kingdom built up an empire around the world. The British Empire became the Commonwealth as nations became independent. After the Second World War, a shortage of workers led to many different peoples from the Empire and Commonwealth coming to work in Britain.
>
> Afro-Caribbeans (Africans and West Indians), Indians, Pakistanis, Chinese and Bangladeshis settled in the United Kingdom, many of them having fought in the British forces in the Second World War.
>
> Even so, in the 2001 Census, only 7.9 per cent of the United Kingdom's population came from ethnic minorities, and over half of these were born and educated in the United Kingdom.
>
> ### The benefits of multi-ethnic societies
>
> Multi-ethnic societies bring more benefits than problems because:
>
> - there is less chance of war because people of different races and nationalities will get to know and like each other
> - they tend to progress more quickly because new people bring in new ideas and new ways of doing things
> - life is more interesting with a much greater variety of food, music, fashion and entertainment.
>
> ### KEY FACTS
>
> Britain is a multi-ethnic society where racial discrimination is banned. Multi-ethnic societies tend to advance more quickly because they have a greater variety of ideas.

KEY WORD

Multi-ethnic society
many different races and cultures living together in one society.

4.5 Problems of prejudice, discrimination and racism

KEY WORDS

Prejudice believing some people are inferior or superior without even knowing them.

Discrimination putting prejudice into practice and treating people less favourably because of their ethnicity/gender/colour/class.

Racial harmony different ethnic groups living together peacefully.

Racism the belief that some ethnic groups are superior to others.

MAIN FACTS

If a multi-ethnic society is to function well, all people must be treated equally and helped to do their best. If people are prejudiced against ethnic groups, this will not happen. For example, a teacher prejudiced against black children will not help them to do their best, and society will lose out.

The other problem with prejudice is that it is likely to lead to discrimination, for example prejudiced employers not giving jobs to certain groups of people. If groups feel they are being treated unfairly, they will cause problems for society, for example turning to crime because they cannot get jobs.

Promoting racial harmony

The United Kingdom promotes racial harmony to stop prejudice, discrimination and racism. It does this by encouragement (making racial harmony part of the school curriculum), by example (having black judges and cabinet ministers) and by laws. The Race Relations Act 1976 banned all forms of racial discrimination and any attempts to stir up racial hatred.

The Labour Party, the Conservative Party and the Liberal Democrat Party are all opposed to racism and have MPs or candidates from ethnic minorities. They also support the work of the Commission for Racial Equality towards racial harmony.

KEY FACTS

A multi-ethnic society needs equal opportunities and treatment to work, and so prejudice and discrimination cause major problems in such a society. The UK has the Race Relations Act and the Commission for Racial Equality to promote racial harmony.

4.6 Christianity and racial harmony

MAIN FACTS

Christianity teaches that all forms of racism are wrong and that Christians should work to bring about racial harmony. It teaches this because:

- Jesus treated people of different races equally
- St Peter had a vision from God telling him that God has no favourites among the races
- in the Parable of the Good Samaritan, Jesus showed that races who hated each other (as did the Jews and Samaritans) should love each other as neighbours
- God created all races in his image
- all the Christian Churches have made statements recently condemning any form of racism or racial discrimination
- all Christian Churches have members, ministers and priests of all races.

KEY FACTS

Christianity teaches that racism is wrong because of the teachings of the Bible and Churches and the example of Jesus.

Remember
The Christian Church is worldwide and over half the world's population is Christian. This means that more than half the Christian Church is non-white.

Islam and racial harmony

MAIN FACTS

Islam teaches that any form of racism is wrong and that Muslims should work to bring about racial harmony.
They believe this because:

- God made all the races on Earth and so people should give each other equal respect
- Muhammad chose an African as his first prayer caller
- Muhammad said in his last sermon that no race is superior to any other
- Muhammad told Muslims that they are one community who should treat each other as brothers.

KEY FACTS

Islam teaches that racism is wrong because of the teachings of the Qur'an and the example of Muhammad.

Attention

You only need to answer on one religion other than Christianity, so only revise the religion you have been taught.

Judaism and racial harmony

MAIN FACTS

Judaism teaches that racism and racial discrimination are completely wrong, and that all Jews should work to bring about racial harmony. They believe this because:

- of the terrible racism which Jews have suffered (e.g. the Holocaust where millions of Jews were killed solely for racist reasons)
- the Torah bans any ill-treatment of other races
- most Jewish rabbis have pointed out that because all people are descendants from Adam, all people are brothers and sisters and so equal in God's sight.

KEY FACTS

Judaism teaches that racism is wrong because of the teachings of the Torah and Jewish experiences in the Holocaust.

Remember

The Holocaust was the attempt by the Nazis to exterminate the Jewish race.

Hinduism and racial harmony

MAIN FACTS

Hinduism is opposed to racism and all forms of racial discrimination. Hindus are expected to work towards racial harmony. They believe this because:

- of the ways Hindus suffered under the Moghul and British Empires
- although the concept of the caste system may appear racist, British Hindus see it as a way of treating everyone with respect
- most Hindus believe that every soul is an actual or potential part of the divine (Brahman), which means that everyone should have equal value and equal treatment.

KEY FACTS

Hindus believe that racism is wrong because every soul is a part of Brahman.

Remember

The Moghul Empire was a Muslim Empire which ruled India from 1526 to about 1800.

Sikhism and racial harmony

MAIN FACTS

Sikhism is opposed to all forms of racism. It does not regard any race as superior and Sikhs in the UK work with other ethnic groups to promote racial harmony.

Sikhs should promote racial harmony because:

- all the Gurus opposed divisions based on caste or race
- Guru Nanak said anyone can come to salvation
- the langar shows that all people and races are treated equally
- there is only one God who created all humanity so all people are brothers and sisters.

KEY FACTS

Sikhism teaches that racism is wrong because of the teachings of the Guru Granth Sahib and the teachings and examples of the Gurus.

Remember

At every Sikh act of worship, there is a free meal in the langar where everyone sits and eats together whatever their race or sex.

MAIN FACTS

Many societies were mono-faith (having only one religion) until the twentieth century, but Britain has had believers in different faiths for many years – Protestants and Catholics from the sixteenth century, and Jews from the seventeenth century.

This led to laws allowing freedom of religion. By the middle of the nineteenth century members of any religion were free to worship and had equal political rights.

In the twentieth century Muslims, Hindus, Sikhs, Buddhists and other religions settled in the United Kingdom, so that it became a truly multi-faith society.

KEY FACTS

Britain is a multi-faith society because several religions are practised in Britain and everyone is free to practise their religion.

KEY WORD

Multi-faith society many different religions living together in one society.

MAIN FACTS

The benefits of living in a multi-faith society

A multi-faith society has many benefits:

- It increases tolerance and understanding as people realise that everyone is entitled to their own opinion on religion.
- It gives people an insight into different religions.
- It makes believers think seriously about their own beliefs.
- It has to have religious freedom which may help to stop religious conflicts.

Any multi-faith society has to give equal rights to all religions, and to people who do not believe in religion. No religion can be thought of as the only true one. Everyone can choose or reject any religion, including their parents' religion.

The problem of having a multi-faith society

Conversion – Many religions (especially Christianity and Islam) think they have a duty to convert other religions. However, religious people attempting to convert each other could be a form of discrimination; they are saying the members of the other faith are not as good as they are. This can also lead to arguments and fights between religions.

Bringing up children – A multi-faith society needs children to learn about all religions, and have the freedom to choose whatever religion they want when they are old enough to think for themselves. They also need the right to reject religion if they want, but most religious parents do not like this, as they want their children to be the same religion as them.

Mixed marriages – In a multi-faith society, young people of different religions are going to meet and want to marry each other. This causes problems for parents and religious leaders:

- Which religious wedding ceremony will they have?
- Which religion will their children be brought up in?

KEY FACTS

A multi-faith society has many benefits such as religious freedom and the opportunity to find out about, and think more deeply about, different religions. It needs to have laws giving equal rights to all religions and to those who have no religion (religious pluralism). However, a multi-faith society can raise problems for religious people in areas such as conversion, bringing up children and mixed marriages.

KEY WORDS

Religious freedom the right to practise your religion and change your religion.

Religious pluralism accepting all religions as having an equal right to co-exist.

Remember

If all religions are equal, no one religion can have all the truth.

MAIN FACTS

All Christian Churches teach that there should be religious freedom – everyone should have the right to follow whatever religion they want. They also teach that people should not be discriminated against because of their religion. However, there are three different Christian attitudes to other religions.

1. Some Christians believe that people can come to God through different religions, but only Christianity has the full truth, and only Christians can be certain that they will go to heaven.

   They believe this because:
   - the Bible says that salvation (going to heaven) comes through believing in Jesus
   - although God can be found in other religions, the full truth about God can only be seen in his son, Jesus.

2. Others believe that Christianity is the only way to come to God and that all other religions are wrong.
   They believe this because:
   - Jesus said that he was the only way to God ('I am the way, the truth and the life. No-one comes to the Father except through me.' John 14:6).

3. Some Christians believe that all religions are equal and that they are just different ways of finding God. So each person should follow the religion they feel most at home with.
   They believe this because:
   - they do not regard the Bible as the word of God
   - they believe that God is a force like gravity which can be discovered by humans in different ways.

KEY FACTS

All Christians believe in religious freedom, but:
- some Christians believe there is some truth in other religions, but only Christianity has the whole truth
- some Christians believe Christianity is the only true religion
- some Christians believe all religions are a path to God.

Remember

'Christian attitudes towards other religions' means what Christians think about non-Christian religions.

Islam and other religions

MAIN FACTS

The Qur'an teaches that there should be no compulsion in religion and so all Muslims believe that people should be free to practise whatever religious faith they choose. However, there are two different attitudes to other religions among Muslims.

1. **Most Muslims** believe that only Islam has God's true message and that everyone should be converted to Islam. They also believe that Muslims cannot change their religion. They believe this because:
   - God dictated the Qur'an to Muhammad and it contains his last complete message on how to live
   - the Qur'an says that only Muslims will go to heaven
   - the Qur'an says that Muslims who give up the faith deserve to die.

2. **A few Muslims** believe that all religions are just different paths to the same God. They believe this because:
   - the Qur'an implies that Jews and Christians have some of the truth about God
   - the Qur'an says there should be no compulsion in religion.

KEY FACTS

All Muslims believe in religious freedom, but:
- some believe that only Islam has the truth
- some believe that God can be found in all religions.

Attention
You only need to answer on one religion other than Christianity, so only revise the religion you have been taught.

Remember
People of the Book is the name for Jews and Christians in the Qur'an.

Judaism and other religions

MAIN FACTS

Jews believe strongly in religious freedom and everyone's right to worship God in the way he or she wishes. There are two attitudes to other religions in Judaism.

1. **Most Jews** believe that all religions are on the path to God if they follow teachings similar to the Ten Commandments. They do not try to convert people from other faiths and do not think other faiths have the right to convert them.
   They believe this because:
   - the Tenakh teaches that all nations will come to God
   - the rabbis teach that following the Noachide Code brings people to God.
2. **Some Jews** believe only Judaism has the truth and they have a right to convert others. They believe this because:
   - the Torah says the Jewish people were especially chosen to bring the world to God.

KEY FACTS

All Jews believe in religious freedom, but:
- some Jews believe all religions are paths to God
- some Jews believe only Judaism has the truth.

(!)

Remember

The Noachide Code is a list of Jewish teachings similar to the Ten Commandments.

Hinduism and other religions

MAIN FACTS

There are two different attitudes to other religions in Hinduism.

1. **Most Hindus** believe that all religions have value and so there should be complete freedom of religion. They believe this because:
   - they see all religions as simply different ways of approaching the same God
   - they see parts of other religions in Hinduism.
2. **Some Hindus** believe that there should be freedom of religion, but only Hinduism has the path to moksha. They believe this because:
   - it is the teaching of the caste system and dharma.

KEY FACTS

All Hindus believe in religious freedom, but:
- some Hindus believe all religions are paths to the divine
- some Hindus believe Hinduism is the only true religion.

Remember

Most Hindus believe that founders of other religions, such as Buddha and Jesus, were avatars of Hindu gods.

Sikhism and other religions

MAIN FACTS

Sikhs believe everyone has the right to follow any religion they want. However, there are different attitudes in Sikhism to other religions.

1. **Most Sikhs** believe that Sikhism has the truth, but all religions are paths to God. It is the one God who speaks through different religions.

   They have this attitude because:
   - there are writings from Muslims and Hindus in the Guru Granth Sahib
   - when the Punjab had a Sikh government (1801–1839) the ruler gave total religious freedom to Hindus and Muslims as well as Sikhs.

2. **Some Sikhs** believe that Sikhism is the only way to achieve mukti. Therefore, everyone should become Sikh.

   They have this attitude because:
   - as the newest world religion, Sikhism must be the best
   - the Gurus showed Hinduism and Islam to be wrong.

KEY FACTS

All Sikhs believe in religious freedom, but:
- some Sikhs believe only Sikhism has the truth
- most Sikhs believe God can be found in all religions.

(!)

Remember

'Sikh attitudes to other religions' means what Sikhs think about non-Sikh religions.

PRACTICE QUESTIONS ✓

a What is a multi-faith society? (2 marks)

b Choose ONE religion, other than Christianity, and outline different attitudes to the roles of men and women in that religion. (6 marks)

c Explain how following Christian teachings may help to prevent racism. (8 marks)

d 'You should only marry someone from your own religion.' Do you agree? Give reasons for your opinion, showing you have considered another point of view. (4 marks)

SECTION
5.1

Religion and the Media

5.1.1 The variety and range of specifically religious programmes

MAIN FACTS

A specifically religious programme is a factual programme about religion and religious issues. These are the programmes that television companies describe as religious broadcasts to the authorities.

There is a wide range and variety of religious programmes.

Worship-type programmes

These are programmes which either broadcast a service, include a lot of hymns or are mainly prayers and readings from religious books. The main programmes of this type are: *Songs of Praise* on BBC1 and the *Sunday Service* on ITV. Many channels also have special worship-type programmes for Lent, Easter, Christmas, Ramadan, Diwali and Jewish New Year.

Magazine-type programmes

These show a mixture of religious news, reviews and interviews. For example, BBC1's main Sunday morning religious programme is *The Heaven and Earth Show*, which is like a religious daytime television magazine-type programme.

Religious documentaries

These are the most popular religious programmes, apart from *Songs of Praise*, and concentrate on religious and moral issues which are investigated in a much deeper way. BBC1 has a regular religious documentary: *Everyman*. Channel 4 has a regular midweek religious documentary screened at prime time: *Witness*. There are also one-off religious documentaries on particular religious issues, such as fundamentalism in different religions.

KEY FACTS

There is a wide range of religious broadcasts on television from the very religious worship-type programmes, such as *Songs of Praise*, to those dealing with religious issues in magazine-type programmes, such as *The Heaven and Earth Show*, and documentaries, such as *Witness*.

Remember

Religious broadcasts are factual programmes about religion and religious issues.
Soap operas with religious themes and sitcoms like *The Vicar of Dibley* are **not** religious broadcasts.

5.1.2 One religious programme in depth

Remember

People can study the National Press instead of soap operas, so the questions say **either** soap operas **or** the National Press. Do not be tempted to answer on the press when you have studied soap operas – you will get a lower mark!

> ## MAIN FACTS
>
> One question will ask you to describe a religious programme. You will need to do the following:
> 1. Write an outline of the contents of the programme.
> 2. Explain why you think it had these contents.
> 3. Explain who would like it and why.
> 4. Explain who would not like it and why.

5.1.3 Soap operas and religious and moral issues

> ## MAIN FACTS
>
> A religious issue is an issue about the meaning of life, or some religious belief about which people argue. For example:
> - Is there life after death?
> - Should priests be able to marry?
> - Should Muslim girls be free to marry anyone they like?
>
> A moral issue is an argument about whether an action is right or wrong. For example:
> - Is it right to divorce when you have young children?
> - Is it ever right to have an abortion?
> - Is it ever right to help a dying person die peacefully?
>
> Moral issues are often religious issues and you should use what you have studied in sections 1–4 in your answers.
>
> Soap operas often explore religious and moral issues:
> - *EastEnders* – when Dot Cotton was asked to help Ethel to die because she was in so much pain from her cancer, Dot struggled with her religious beliefs, before helping Ethel to die.
> - *Coronation Street* – when Todd realised he was gay and left his pregnant girlfriend, Sarah, she went into early labour and the baby was stillborn; the religious issues of the death of babies and blame and forgiveness were explored.
>
> All soaps find moral issues a great source of story lines – sex outside marriage, abortion, euthanasia, commitment, racism, mixed marriages, etc. are covered regularly.
>
> ### KEY FACTS
>
> Soap operas deal with many religious issues (such as life after death and mixed marriages) and many moral issues (such as adultery, abortion and euthanasia). These issues are important parts of life, and soap operas are about life. You should think about whether soap operas are a good way of dealing with such issues.

5.1.4 An in-depth study of one such issue

MAIN FACTS

Refer to one issue you have watched in a soap and do the following:

1. Name the soap.
2. Name the issue.
3. Name the main characters involved.
4. Describe how this issue was dealt with.
5. Explain why you think the soap dealt with this issue in this way.
6. Identify other ways in which this issue could have been dealt with.
7. Explain how you would have dealt with this issue and why.
8. Explain whether you think a soap opera was a good way of dealing with this issue.

5.1.5 Religious themes in film and television dramas

MAIN FACTS

A religious theme is anything to do with religion such as living in a multi-faith society, women priests, etc.

Edexcel is not strict on what a television drama is. Sitcoms, such as *The Vicar of Dibley*, and 'serious cartoons', such as *The Simpsons* will be accepted. However, documentaries, soap operas or religious broadcasts will receive zero marks.
There are many films and dramas for you to choose from.

Films

Sister Act is a film with a religious theme of worship. Whoopi Goldberg hides in a convent when escaping from the Mafia. The convent church has a very small congregation until Whoopi makes the worship more exciting and it becomes packed.

Other films which have a religious theme are:

- *Bend it Like Beckham* – the problems for Sikh parents in bringing up their children in a multi-faith society;
- *Keeping the Faith* – Jewish–Catholic relations and whether priests should marry;
- *Chocolat* – the problems caused by Catholics who are very strict about their religion.

Remember

It must be a religious theme and you should make it clear in your answer what the religious theme is.

Television dramas

Many television dramas have religious themes. *William and Mary* was a drama series about a midwife and an undertaker falling in love. The life and death issues they faced at work were often connected with religion.

The Vicar of Dibley was a sitcom which dealt with the religious theme of women priests in the Church of England.

An episode of *Red Dwarf (The Last Day)* dealt with the religious theme of life after death and whether society uses it to keep people in their place.

Many episodes of *The Simpsons* have a religious theme.

You should use some of this material when answering evaluation questions on the media.

Remember

It must be a religious theme and you should make it clear in your answer what the religious theme is.

5.1.6 A study of a religious theme in a film

MAIN FACTS

Make a list of the following for whichever film or television drama you have chosen:

1. The name of the film or television drama.
2. The religious theme.
3. Why the theme is important.
4. Why you think it was chosen.
5. How the theme was dealt with in the film or television drama.
6. Whether you think this was a good way to deal with the theme. Remember to give your reasons.
7. Whether the treatment was fair to religious people. Use examples from the film or television drama to show this, for example '*East is East* was not fair to Muslims because the father was supposed to be a typical Muslim, but he was not because...'.

Remember

DO NOT use soap operas, religious broadcasts, or documentaries.

5.1.7 How religion is dealt with by the media

MAIN FACTS

It is very important that you think carefully about evaluation questions on Religion and the Media.

- A question such as '"Religious programmes are boring." Do you agree?' means that you should only look at religious programmes (worship- and magazine-type programmes and religious documentaries). You must not use soap operas, films or any other television programmes as examples. There need to be religious programmes because religion is an important part of British life. More people go to church on Sunday than go to watch football matches on Saturday and about 75 per cent of the population of England and Wales claimed to have a religion in the 2001 census.

- Questions that refer to religion on television or in the media mean that you can write about all types of programmes that have anything to do with religion. This means that you need to sort out whether what you have seen of the treatment of religion is fair and gives a true picture of religion. It might be a good idea to sort these out into two columns:

Programmes giving a fair, true picture	Programmes giving an unfair, untrue picture

Remember, you will need actual examples of the programmes.

- In any evaluation question you must use examples from specific programmes or films to back up the points you make.

Remember

Questions that refer to the treatment of religion in the media (or on television) mean you can write about all types of programmes and films that have anything to do with religion.

Remember

You must refer to specific programmes in your answers.

PRACTICE QUESTIONS ✓

a Outline the variety and range of specifically religious programmes on television. (4 marks)

b Choose a religious theme from a film or television drama (NOT a soap opera) and explain how this theme was dealt with. (8 marks)

c 'Television soap operas offer a good way of dealing with religious and moral issues.'
Do you agree? Give reasons for your opinion, showing you have considered another point of view. (8 marks)

5.2 Religion: Wealth and Poverty

5.2.1 Christian teachings on wealth

MAIN FACTS

Christians believe that wealth itself is not bad because it can be used for good (such as buying food for the starving) as well as evil.

However, the Bible shows that if people have the wrong attitude to money it can lead them away from God. In the Parable of the Rich Fool (Luke 12:13–21), Jesus told a story about a farmer who made lots of money and thought he would be able to 'eat, drink and be merry', but he died that night with no chance to enjoy his wealth.

Jesus taught that people should not try to get wealth in this life, but should try to make themselves rich in religion.

The Christian Church teaches that Christians have a duty to make money for themselves and their families to live, but only in lawful and moral ways. Christians should not be involved in businesses that hurt people, such as the sex industry and the gambling industry. When working for an employer, Christians should work fairly and honestly. When working for themselves, Christians should treat their employees fairly and never try to cheat customers.

KEY FACTS

Christianity teaches that wealth itself is neither bad nor good, but the way it is used can be bad. Christians should not seek money for its own sake. Money is needed to provide a decent standard of living for their families, but Christians must make it honestly and use it fairly in Christian ways.

(!)

Remember
The love of money makes people do evil things, according to the Bible.

Muslim teachings on wealth

MAIN FACTS

Islam teaches that wealth is something given by God for the good of everyone, therefore it is something to be shared.

Islam says that Muslims have a duty to make money to provide for themselves and their families, but they should only gain money in lawful and moral ways. Muslims should not be involved with alcohol or gambling, nor with industries that hurt people, such as the sex industry.

When working for an employer, Muslims should work fairly and honestly. When working for themselves, Muslims should treat their employees fairly, never try to cheat customers and not charge interest.

KEY FACTS

Islam teaches that wealth is a gift from God to make life better. Muslims have a duty to make the money that is needed to provide a decent standard of living for their families, but they must make it honestly and use it fairly having nothing to do with charging interest, alcohol or gambling.

Attention
You only need to answer on one religion other than Christianity, so only revise the religion you have been taught.

Jewish teachings on wealth

MAIN FACTS

Judaism teaches that wealth is a gift from God to make life better for oneself and for others.

Judaism teaches that Jews have a duty to make money to provide for themselves and their families, but they should only make money in lawful and moral ways. Jews should not be involved in businesses that hurt people, such as the sex industry, or that want them to work on Friday evenings or Saturdays.

When working for an employer, Jews should work fairly and honestly. When working for themselves, Jews should treat their employees fairly and never try to cheat customers.

KEY FACTS

Judaism teaches that wealth is a gift from God to make life better. Jews have a duty to make the money that is needed to provide a decent standard of living for their families, but they must make it honestly and use it fairly following the mitzvot.

Remember
Sabbath lasts from sunset Friday to sunset Saturday and Orthodox Jews must do no work on the Sabbath.

Hindu teachings on wealth

MAIN FACTS

Hindus believe that wealth is a good thing if it has been gained by lawful means.

Hinduism teaches that Hindus have a duty to make money to provide for themselves and their families, but they should only work in jobs where they can follow their dharma (social duty) in their ashrama (stage of life) without hurting people or animals.

When working for an employer, Hindus should work fairly and honestly. When working for themselves, Hindus should treat their employees fairly and never try to cheat customers.

KEY FACTS

Hinduism teaches that wealth is a good thing, which people should enjoy if it is part of their dharma. Hindus have a duty to make the money that is needed to provide a decent standard of living for their families, but they must make it honestly and use it fairly.

Remember

The Arthashastra is a holy book about how Hindus should use wealth.

Sikh teachings on wealth

MAIN FACTS

Sikhs believe that wealth and possessions are a gift from God, but wealth can make people manmukh (self/human-centred), so Sikhs must be very careful about wealth.

Sikhism says that Sikhs have a duty to make money to provide for themselves and their families, but should only gain money in lawful and moral ways. Sikhs should not be involved with alcohol or gambling, nor with industries which hurt people, such as the sex industry.

When working for an employer, Sikhs should work fairly and honestly. When working for themselves, Sikhs should treat their employees fairly and never try to cheat customers.

KEY FACTS

Sikhism teaches that wealth is a gift from God, which must not be used to make people manmukh. Sikhs can be wealthy, and have a duty to make the money that is needed to provide a decent standard of living for their families, but they must make it honestly and use it fairly.

Remember

If Sikhs are self-centred, they cannot achieve release from rebirth (mukti).

5.2.3 Christian teachings on stewardship and the relief of poverty

MAIN FACTS

Christianity teaches that God made humans the stewards of the Earth and its resources. In the Parable of the Talents or Minas (Luke 19:11–26), Jesus taught that Christians should leave the Earth better than they found it.

The Churches teach that stewardship means looking after the Earth's resources, and sharing them fairly.

The New Testament teaches that riches must be used to help the poor.

Jesus told the Parable of the Sheep and the Goats about the good and bad people being sorted out at the end of the world. The good would be sent to heaven because they had helped the poor and starving. The bad people were told they were going to hell because they had never helped the poor and starving. He said helping the poor and starving was like helping him (based on Matthew 25:31–46). Clearly this means that Christians should help to relieve world poverty.

Jesus taught in the Sermon on the Mount that Christians should use their wealth to help those in need, and all the Christian Churches say that Christians have a duty to help the poor.

So Christian teachings on stewardship and the relief of poverty mean that Christians should help remove world poverty and promote world development.

KEY FACTS

Christianity teaches that Christians are stewards of the Earth and hold their possessions on behalf of God and so should share with the poor. The teachings of Jesus and the Churches say that Christians must use their money to help remove poverty and suffering.

Remember

The Sermon on the Mount is the main teaching Jesus gave about how Christians should behave.

Islam and stewardship

MAIN FACTS

Islam teaches that God made Adam as his khalifah (steward) to look after the Earth for him. This means that Muslims have to look after the people of the Earth as well as its resources. This means making sure the good things of the Earth are shared out fairly. This is very important because Muslims believe that, at the end of the world, they will be judged by God on whether they have been good stewards.

Sharing wealth is commanded by God in the pillar of Zakah. Many Muslims believe that giving Zakah purifies the money they have left so that no harm can come to them from it.

Muslims should pay two and a half per cent of all their savings as Zakah every year.

Islam also teaches that Muslims should give to charity if they are ever asked, or if they have any spare cash. They are also taught to help the poor by giving interest-free loans.

British Muslims often send their Zakah to help the poor in less economically developed countries (LEDCs). Often a mosque in Pakistan asks a British mosque to help with things like wells and medical work.

So the teachings on stewardship and the relief of poverty mean that Muslims should help remove world poverty and promote world development. They do this through charities such as Muslim Aid and Islamic Relief, which help people in LEDCs.

KEY FACTS

Islam teaches that Muslims are stewards of the Earth (khalifah) and hold their possessions on behalf of God and so should share with the poor. The teachings of Zakah and the Qur'an say that Muslims must use their money to help remove poverty and suffering.

Attention

You only need to answer on one religion other than Christianity, so only revise the religion you have been taught.

Remember

Zakah is a tax Muslims must pay to help the poor. Sadaqah is extra giving to the poor.

Judaism and stewardship

MAIN FACTS

Judaism teaches that God created the universe, so Jews should treat creation as a gift from God to be used by humans in the way in which God intended.

Judaism teaches that God made humans the stewards of the Earth and its resources. So they must look after it and pass it on to the next generation. Judaism teaches that God's stewards must use the Earth's resources fairly as well as wisely.

The Torah says Jews must give one tenth of their income to the poor as tzedaka (charity or correctness). By giving to the poor people, Jews are using money correctly to put the poor into their correct position in society.

Maimonides (a famous Jewish thinker) taught that the best form of charity makes sure that the poor will never need charity again. Many rabbis taught that giving charity puts people right with God, so their prayers are accepted. This is why there is a charity box in every synagogue.

Every Jewish home should also have a charity box so that at times of celebration or good fortune the family can thank God by putting money in.

These teachings on stewardship and the relief of poverty mean that Jews should help remove world poverty and promote world development. They do this through specific Jewish charities such as World Jewish Relief, and by helping non-religious charities such as Oxfam and the Save the Children Fund.

KEY FACTS

Judaism teaches that Jews are stewards of the Earth and hold their possessions on behalf of God and so should share with the poor. The teachings of the Torah and Talmud (especially on tzedaka) say that Jews must use their money to help remove poverty and suffering.

Remember

There are lots of teachings in the Tenakh about how Jews should help the poor.

Hinduism and stewardship

MAIN FACTS

Hindus are taught that there is a oneness in the universe and nature, so God is a part of the Earth. Hindus should therefore protect nature and respect all forms of life.

Hinduism teaches that all people have part of God within them, so by helping poor people, Hindus will be helping the divine. Many Hindus believe that helping the poor brings good karma, which will help to gain moksha. Any Hindu refusing to help the poor will gain bad karma and not gain moksha.

All Hindu temples collect charity gifts, which are used either to help poor Hindus in Britain or to help projects in India.

These teachings mean that Hindus should help to relieve poverty especially in less developed countries. Many of the schemes established in India to help the poor have been set up by Hindus. Many Hindu groups organise relief work in India trying to end poverty.

KEY FACTS

Hinduism teaches that there is a oneness in the universe and so Hindus should share with the poor to find oneness, God and peace. The teachings on karma mean that Hindus should use their money to help remove poverty and suffering as a way of gaining moksha.

Remember

Moksha is the release from rebirth that all Hindus are aiming for.

Sikhism and stewardship

MAIN FACTS

The Guru Granth Sahib teaches that God is a part of the Earth, therefore all forms of life are to be respected. So Sikhs have a duty to look after the Earth.

Sikhism teaches that all people have part of God within them, so by helping poor people, Sikhs will be helping God. Many Sikhs believe that helping the poor brings good karma which will help to gain mukti. Any Sikh refusing to help the poor will be manmukh and find it hard to gain mukti.

All the human Gurus and the Guru Granth Sahib make it very clear that Sikhs should help the poor. The Rahit Maryada suggests that Sikhs should give ten per cent of their wealth to charity.

These teachings mean that Sikhs should help to relieve poverty especially in less developed countries. So British Sikhs support Sikh charities in the Punjab and also non-religious charities such as Oxfam and the Save the Children Fund.

KEY FACTS

Sikhism teaches that as God is part of the Earth, and all life is to be respected, Sikhs should share their possessions with the poor. The teachings of the Guru Granth Sahib and the examples of the Gurus mean Sikhs should use their money to help remove poverty and suffering.

Remember
The Punjab is the area in North West India where Sikhism began.

5.2.5 The causes of world poverty

MAIN FACTS

World poverty is very complicated. The countries of the West (e.g. the USA, France and the UK) are regarded as rich, the countries of the East (e.g. Bangladesh and India) are regarded as poor. But things are constantly changing. Some countries go from poor to rich (e.g. Brunei), some from poor to less poor (e.g. Malaysia), some from less poor to poor (e.g. Zimbabwe). Countries are often classed as:

- **MEDC** – more economically developed (e.g. USA) – First World
- **EDC** – economically developing (e.g. Mexico) – Second World
- **LEDC** – less economically developed (e.g. Bangladesh) – Third World

The main causes of world poverty are:

Wars

Many LEDCs suffer from wars. These are sometimes caused by corruption, or by the way the country was split up when colonised by Europeans in the nineteenth century, creating 'artificial countries'. Artificial countries often have civil wars between different ethnic groups, as happened in Kosovo and Serbia in Europe.

Wars destroy crops, homes, schools and hospitals and create refugees. A neighbouring country can often move from developing to less developed when war refugees arrive needing shelter, food, etc.

Natural disasters

Many LEDCs are in areas where there are regular natural disasters like earthquakes and floods which can destroy homes, farmland, etc. Bangladesh has bad floods almost every year.

Debt

All LEDCs suffer from debt. They have to borrow money from banks in developed countries and pay large amounts of interest to the bank, which they could have spent on development. Because unpaid interest is added to the debt, the amount of interest poor countries have to pay rich countries has gone up from £7.4 billion to £10.3 billion since 1990.

Remember

An artificial country is one where the boundaries ignore the nationality of the people so that the same nation can be in two different countries.

Unfair trade

The rich countries organise world trade.

Many LEDCs try to get money from abroad by growing and selling crops. But the rich countries pay their farmers grants (subsidies) to grow crops and put high taxes on the crops from LEDCs so their goods are expensive. Then they export the crops their farmers have grown at prices less than the LEDCs can grow them for.

The rich countries pay $350 billion in subsidies to rich farmers and $57 billion in aid to LEDCs. Many countries try to solve this by growing cash crops (cotton, tea, coffee, etc.) to sell to the MEDCs, but this uses land that could have grown food, leading to starvation.

AIDS/HIV

This disease is spreading rapidly in LEDCs because they cannot afford condoms and drugs. A quarter of the children in South Africa will have lost their parents to the disease by 2010. This is removing workers and destroying the economy. Only the rich countries can help.

Other factors

There are also problems of lack of clean water, too many children, lack of education, etc., which prevent countries from developing.

KEY FACTS

The main causes of world poverty are:
- natural disasters
- wars
- debt
- lack of education
- overpopulation
- lack of investment.

!

Remember

Overpopulation means there are too many children in a country to be supported by the income of the country.

5.2.6 The need for world development

MAIN FACTS

The world is now interdependent (we all rely on each other), so world poverty concerns us all. About 1.2 billion people live on less than $1 a day, but countries like the USA and the UK have obesity (being too overweight) problems. Hundreds of millions are starving and millions of children get no education. The only way to stop this unfairness is world development.

1. The Universal Declaration of Human Rights of the United Nations says:
   - All human beings are born free and equal and should act towards one another like brothers. (Article 1)
   - Everyone has the right to enough food, clothing, housing and medical care. (Article 25)
   - Everyone has the right to free elementary education. (Article 26)

   If the United Nations thinks these are basic human rights, everyone should work for world development to bring them about.

2. The rich nations rely on the poor nations for essentials like copper, uranium, coffee and tea. If the poor nations do not get a fair price, they may stop making them.

3. The world works on the system of capitalism, where people are free to set up companies and sell things that they think people want to buy. This system relies on people having money to buy what is made. This means the MEDCs actually need the poorer countries to have more money so they can buy their goods.

4. If poor countries do not think they are getting a fair deal, they may turn to violence against the rich. World development is a way to bring world peace.

KEY FACTS

The world needs Less Economically Developed Countries to develop so that they can buy goods and services from the More Economically Developed Countries. Otherwise, trade will stop and no one's lives will improve.

(!)

Remember

The United Nations is an organisation of most of the countries in the world set up to promote peace, security and cooperation.

5.2.7 The work of one religious agency for world development

MAIN FACTS

Christian Aid was founded by the British Council of Churches after 1945 to help those left homeless after the Second World War. Its aim is to provide help where the need is greatest. Today, Christian Aid works alongside 570 partner organisations in the developing world because it believes local groups are best placed to find their own solutions to the problems they face.

Christian Aid:

- raises funds in Britain through Churches, particularly during Christian Aid Week, which raised £15 million in 2004
- provides long-term aid to help poor people become self-sufficient, e.g. helping Health Unlimited in Cambodia to provide basic health education to communities devastated by war
- provides aid for emergencies such as floods, earthquakes and wars
- campaigns to remove the causes of poverty such as unfair trade and unjust debts
- educates people in Britain so that they realise why there is a need to raise funds for and help people in the developing world.

How Christian Aid tries to remove the causes of world poverty

- Natural Disasters – Christian Aid sends emergency supplies to deal with the effects of earthquakes, floods, volcanoes, etc.
- Wars – Christian Aid works in local communities to help them find peaceful solutions together with the United Nations and other groups trying to bring peace.
- Debt – Christian Aid was one the leaders of Jubilee 2000 trying to persuade world leaders to cancel the debts of LEDCs.
- Education – Christian Aid funds schools and teachers in LEDCs.
- Health – Christian Aid helps to set up clinics and hospitals. It also works to provide clean water and health advice.
- Lack of food – Christian Aid is providing training in new farming methods and ways of preventing desertification, etc.

Remember
Christian Aid tries to stop the bad effects of natural disasters by sending emergency supplies.

Remember
Christian Aid tries to remove war by working with groups trying to bring peace.

Remember
Christian Aid tries to remove debt by persuading MEDC governments to cancel the debts of LEDCs.

Remember
Christian Aid tries to remove ignorance by funding schools and teachers in LEDCs.

Remember
Christian Aid tries to remove starvation by training LEDCs in new farming methods and ways of preventing desertification.

Christian Aid was founded by the Christian Churches. It helps LEDCs and aims to remove the causes of world poverty. It raises funds in the UK to fund groups in LEDCs who are working to develop their countries, e.g. working with the Council of Churches in Burundi to help young Tutsis and Hutus to live in peace together.

5.2.8 Evaluation issues on wealth and poverty

MAIN FACTS

You will need to be aware of non-religious ideas in order to answer evaluation questions:

1. You will need to be aware of what governments are doing. The United Nations Human Development Report of 2003 (a scheme to halve world poverty by 2015) says that the best way to promote world development is through government action. It claims that if rich governments stopped subsidising their farmers and increased their aid to LEDCs whose governments treat their citizens decently, stay out of wars and promote equality, literacy and health, then poverty could be halved.

2. You also need to be aware that there are non-religious aid agencies doing as much as religious agencies. Oxfam is a non-religious British agency which raises more money and funds more development work than Christian Aid (in 2002–03 Christian Aid spent £42.9 million on development work; Oxfam spent £114.9 million).

3. You also need to be aware that world development is happening. According to United Nations figures, 30 per cent of the world's population were living in extreme poverty in 1990, but by 1999 that had reduced to 23 per cent.

KEY FACTS

World development is happening and there are many fewer people living in poverty today than ten years ago. Perhaps the best way to end world poverty is government action, especially for rich governments to stop subsidising their farmers. There are as many non-religious as religious organisations doing much for world development.

PRACTICE QUESTIONS ✓

a Outline the causes of world poverty. (4 marks)

b Explain how one religious agency is trying to remove the causes of world poverty. (8 marks)

c 'Only religious organisations can solve world poverty.' Do you agree? Give reasons for your opinion, showing you have considered another point of view. (8 marks)

FULL MARK ANSWERS TO PRACTICE QUESTIONS

BELIEVING IN GOD

This would gain full marks because it is a clear and correct definition.

a What is a miracle? (2 marks)
An event that seems to break a law of nature and which can only be explained as an act of God.

b Describe a religious experience. (6 marks)

This would gain full marks because it is a coherent description of a religious experience, which is clearly identified as religious.

A religious experience occurred when I was in hospital in Austria. I had a bad accident and I remember seeing everything that I had done flash before me. The problem was that I was myself and yet I did not feel as though I was myself. I remember the lights growing dim and I felt as though I was at one with the world. It was very calm and peaceful and I remember everything turning hazy. I felt I was with God. A religious experience makes you feel God is real.

c Choose ONE religion and explain how its followers respond to the problem of evil and suffering. (8 marks)

This would gain full marks because it is a comprehensive and coherent explanation which gives four reasons to explain how Christians respond to evil and suffering. It uses specialist vocabulary appropriately (prayer, Christian Aid, benevolent, omnipotent, free will, souls, heaven).

Christians respond to the problem of evil and suffering in several ways. The main way is through trying to get rid of evil and suffering. So Christians respond to the problem by praying for those who suffer and trying to help them through groups like Christian Aid. Christians also try to explain how God can be benevolent (good) and omnipotent (all-powerful) and still allow evil and suffering to exist. One way they do this is to claim that humans were given free will by God to prepare their souls for heaven. This means that evil and suffering are the fault of humans misusing their free will and not the fault of God. Many Christians also respond by saying they do not know why there is evil and suffering, but God is greater than us and must have his reasons which we, as humans, cannot understand.

d 'No one can be sure that God exists.'
Do you agree? Give reasons for your opinion, showing you have considered another point of view. (4 marks)

This would gain full marks because it gives an alternative point of view with reasons, then it says what is wrong with that point of view in order to come to a personal opinion with a reason. It uses religious reasons and specialist vocabulary (Bible, religious experiences, benevolent, omnipotent).

Some people might disagree with this statement because they are Christians who are sure that God exists. They believe this because they believe the Bible is a book written by God and so God must exist. They may also be sure because of their own religious experiences such as praying for someone who has cancer who is later cured. This makes them sure that God exists because he answered their prayers.

However, I think they are wrong and I would agree with this statement. There is no evidence that the Bible came from God and their friend who had cancer might have recovered anyway, despite their prayers. I think there is no scientific evidence that God exists, and things such as evil and suffering make it seem that there can be no God because a benevolent and omnipotent God would not let such things happen. So I agree with this statement.

MATTERS OF LIFE AND DEATH

This would gain full marks because it is the correct definition.

a What is euthanasia? (2 marks)

A gentle or easy death.

b Choose ONE religion, other than Christianity, and outline its teachings about euthanasia. (6 marks)

This would gain full marks because it is a coherent outline of all Muslim teachings about euthanasia.

Islam teaches that euthanasia is completely wrong. It does not allow any form of euthanasia because all life is in the hands of Allah and only he can decide when someone should die. Islam teaches that this life is a test and euthanasia is a form of cheating in the test. However, some Muslims believe that switching off life-support machines is allowed because the person's brain has died, so it is not euthanasia.

c Explain why there are different beliefs among Christians about life after death. (8 marks)

This would gain full marks because it is a comprehensive and coherent explanation which outlines two different beliefs, gives two reasons for each belief and concludes with a general reason. It uses specialist vocabulary appropriately (resurrection, Day of Judgement, Jesus, St Paul, Bible, immortality, Gospels, paranormal).

Some Christians believe in the resurrection of the body, which means that when you die nothing happens until the Day of Judgement when you will be raised and given a new body and judged by God. The good go to heaven and the bad go to hell. They believe this because Jesus' body was raised from the dead showing your body will be raised. Also St Paul teaches the resurrection of the body and the Day of Judgement in 1 Corinthians, this is in the Bible, which they believe is the word of God.

Other Christians believe in the immortality of the soul. This means that when you die, your soul lives on and goes to heaven or hell straight away. They believe this because, according to the Gospels, Jesus told the robber on the cross with him that he would go to paradise that day. They also believe this because of the evidence of the paranormal through ghosts and mediums.

So there are different beliefs because Christians interpret the Bible in different ways and have different experiences of life.

d 'Religious people should never have abortions.'
Do you agree? Give reasons for your opinion, showing you have considered another point of view. In your answer, you should refer to at least one religion. (4 marks)

This would gain full marks because it gives an alternative point of view with reasons, then it says what is wrong with that point of view in order to come to a personal opinion with a reason. It uses religious reasons and specialist vocabulary (Roman Catholic, conception, sacred, Ten Commandments, Islam, Protestant).

I can see why people might say this because most religions say that you should not have an abortion. For example, Roman Catholics say that abortion is like murder because life begins at conception. They say that life is sacred and belongs to God and murder is breaking one of the Ten Commandments.

However, this view is wrong because it ignores the evidence from other religions. Islam allows an abortion if the mother's life is in danger. Protestant Christians also allow an abortion if the mother's life is at risk or if the child is the result of rape. So, if there are situations when some religions allow abortion, it cannot be true to say that religious people should never have abortions. Therefore I think the statement is wrong.

MARRIAGE AND THE FAMILY

This would gain full marks because it is the correct definition

a What is cohabitation? (2 marks)

Living together without being married.

b Choose ONE religion, other than Christianity, and outline the purposes of marriage in that religion. (6 marks)

This would gain full marks because it is a coherent outline of three purposes of marriage in Judaism.

Judaism teaches that while it is not the law that Jews should marry, it is expected that they do. This is so that the faith does not die out. Jews believe that marriage is for lawful sex and for a man and a woman to share each other's needs. Marriage is also to have children and bring them up in a Jewish family to continue the faith. Jewish men should marry Jewish women and vice versa.

c Explain why there are different attitudes in Christianity to divorce. (8 marks)

This would gain full marks because it is a comprehensive and coherent explanation which outlines two different attitudes, gives at least two reasons for each attitude and concludes with a general reason. It uses specialist vocabulary appropriately (Roman Catholic, Jesus, Moses, Catechism, marriage vows, Bible, Matthew's Gospel).

Christians have different views about divorce because some Christians allow divorce and some (mainly Roman Catholics) do not allow it. Some Christians do not allow divorce because in the marriage service you promise to stay with your partner until death parts you, and this promise is made to God, so only God can end the marriage. Also Jesus said that divorce had been allowed by Moses, but he thought it was wrong. Also the Catechism of the Catholic Church teaches that divorce is wrong.

Other Christians allow divorce because they believe that Christianity is all about forgiveness and being allowed a second chance by God, so they think people should be allowed to divorce if their marriage has collapsed. They also point to a saying of Jesus in Matthew's Gospel that he allowed divorce in the case of adultery. So there are different attitudes because Christians interpret the Bible and the marriage vows differently.

d 'Living together is better than getting married.'
Do you agree? Give reasons for your opinion, showing you have considered another point of view. In your answer you should refer to at least one religion. (4 marks)

This would gain full marks because it gives an alternative point of view with reasons, then it says what is wrong with that point of view in order to come to a personal opinion with a reason. It uses religious reasons and specialist vocabulary (divorce rate, cohabitation, Christianity, Qur'an, Shari'ah).

I can see why some people might say this. They might look at the high divorce rate and the cost of getting divorced and say that you might just as well live together and it will then be easier if you break up. They will also point to the fact that cohabitation is working for many couples today.

However, I do not agree because no religious person can agree with this. Christianity teaches that if you are in love with someone and want to live with them and have children, you must get married. The Qur'an and Shari'ah teach that, for Muslims, sex should only occur in marriage. I think other religions also say something similar. It must also be the case that it is more stable to be married and it is a better environment for children. After all, one in three marriages ends in divorce, but that means two in three succeed and I do not think living together will have such a high success rate, therefore I disagree with the statement.

SOCIAL HARMONY

This would gain full marks because it gives a clear definition.

a What is a multi-faith society? (2 marks)

A multi-faith society is one where people from different backgrounds, religions and beliefs are living in the same area.

b Choose ONE religion, other than Christianity, and outline different attitudes to the roles of men and women in that religion. (6 marks)

This would gain full marks because it is a coherent outline of two different Muslim attitudes to the roles of men and women.

Traditional Muslims believe that both husband and wife should make sure that their children are brought up as good Muslims. It is the husband's role to provide financially and make sure that the children are given a good Muslim education. It is the wife's role to look after the children and make sure that all the food laws are kept and teach the children to do salah at home. Only men should go to mosque. Modern Muslims believe that husband and wife should have equal roles and that the wife can have a career and should go to mosque.

c Explain how following Christian teachings may help to prevent racism. (8 marks)

This would gain full marks because it is a comprehensive and coherent explanation which outlines four teachings and explains how following each one could help to prevent racism. It uses specialist vocabulary appropriately (Good Samaritan, parable, Jesus, Church of England, Catholic Church).

Christians say God loves anyone from any race because he made everyone and following this teaching should stop racism. The parable of the Good Samaritan teaches Christians that they should not be racist. The parable tells the story of a man who was robbed on a road and needed help, a priest walked past without helping, so did a second Jewish religious leader, but the third (a Samaritan) helped the Jew even though the two races did not like each other. Christians should follow the teaching of Jesus and behave like the Samaritan who was not racist.

Christians also believe in loving their neighbours, which means they cannot be racist, and all the Churches are against racism. The Church of England and the Catholic Church are always making statements saying racism is wrong and that Christians must not be racist. So following Christian teachings should help to prevent racism.

d 'You should only marry someone from your own religion.' Do you agree? Give reasons for your opinion, showing you have considered another point of view. (4 marks)

This would gain full marks because it gives an alternative point of view with reasons, then it says what is wrong with that point of view in order to come to a personal opinion with a reason. It uses religious reasons and specialist vocabulary (Muslim, Christian, heaven, pollute, worship, mixed marriages).

I think some people might agree with this statement because some religions do not want to pollute themselves with having other religions in them. Also problems arise, for example, when a Muslim girl marries a Christian man as it will be unclear which religion the children should follow. There will also be the worry of grandparents that their grandchild will not go to heaven.

However, I think these people are wrong. At the end of the day all religions worship the same God don't they? I mean they might have different ways of worshipping, but it is the same God. Therefore, there can be no polluting and everyone who is good will go to heaven. I think everyone should have the choice to marry the person they love whatever their religion. I am sure mixed marriages can work if you really love each other. Therefore I think the statement is wrong and I disagree with it.

RELIGION AND THE MEDIA

a Outline the variety and range of specifically religious programmes on television. (4 marks)

This would gain full marks because the range and variety of specifically religious programmes is clearly outlined.

There is a wide range of religious broadcasts on television from worship-type programmes such as 'Songs of Praise', through religious magazine and discussion programmes such as 'The Heaven and Earth Show' to religious documentaries such as 'Everyman' on BBC1 and 'Witness' on Channel 4. At special times such as Easter, Diwali and Ramadan there are special programmes.

There is also a great variety within the different types of religious programmes. 'Songs of Praise' is not only hymn-singing; each week has a theme and explores a variety of issues with a variety of people. There are even five different presenters who appeal to different groups of people. The magazine programmes have different issues each week and the discussion programmes have lots of different target audiences giving them a great variety. Documentaries are different every week. Religious broadcasting has a range and a variety to encourage a wide audience.

b Choose a religious theme from a film or television drama (NOT a soap opera) and explain how this theme was dealt with. (8 marks)

This would gain full marks because the way the programme dealt with the theme of miracles is very clearly explained and the effect of the programme on the viewer's understanding of the religious theme is also shown. There is also good use of specialist vocabulary – confession, priest, absolution, Virgin Mary, supernatural, recovery of faith.

The television comedy drama 'Only Fools and Horses' dealt with the religious theme of miracles in the episode 'The Miracle of Peckham'.

The programme dealt with the theme in an amusing, but very thought-provoking way. It began with a very religious situation. Delboy went to church to confess his sins. It was a Roman Catholic church, and the priest wondered how long it would take Delboy to make his confession as he knew he had never been to confession before. Delboy confessed to being involved in buying suspect goods and was given absolution.

The priest began to talk about his doubts about God, because the church hospice was being closed down unless they could raise £1 million and the old and sick would not be able to be near their relatives. As Delboy was leaving the church, the priest saw the statue of the Virgin Mary crying and shouted to Delboy. They both saw it as a miracle and Delboy suggested that by selling the TV and newspaper rights they could raise the money for the hospice.

Later we learn that the suspect goods were the lead from the church roof and the tears of the Virgin were the rain coming through the roof. However, the money for the hospice had been raised by Delboy who did not keep any for himself.

The way this was done made you think about what a miracle is. The supernatural miracle of the statue crying had not happened. However, in a sense a miracle had happened. The money to save the hospice had been raised, something the priest had thought impossible; Delboy had raised money for charity without keeping any for himself and the priest had recovered his faith.

c 'Television soap operas offer a good way of dealing with religious and moral issues.'

Do you agree? Give reasons for your opinion, showing you have considered another point of view. (8 marks)

This would gain full marks because it gives an alternative point of view with reasons, then it says what is wrong with that point of view in order to come to a personal opinion with a reason. It refers very clearly to specific programmes which are used to back up the points made.

Some people might disagree because if a person wants help in making a decision, the character or situation in the soap opera might provoke a wrong decision so that the person makes the same wrong decision. And besides, television soap operas are made up, although some people think they are real, and so the situations are not true to life. They could also upset or put pressure on someone who has been in a similar position to that of the character on television. For example, someone having an abortion in a soap opera might upset someone at home who has had one.

However, I do not agree with these views. Programmes like 'EastEnders', 'Coronation Street' and 'Emmerdale' all deal with religious and moral issues. 'EastEnders' had a good storyline when Dot Cotton was asked to help her friend Ethel to die. Dot was a Christian and the story showed how her religious beliefs conflicted with her love for her friend. I found this storyline very moving and understood more about why euthanasia is an issue for Christians after watching this programme than from reading a textbook on Christianity and euthanasia. 'Coronation Street' deals with adultery and 'Emmerdale' with abortion, murder, under-age sex, and sex outside marriage. These three soap operas alone cover a wide variety of moral issues. 'EastEnders' covers more religious issues because none of the others have characters from other races in them. 'Coronation Street' once had Samir, Deirdre's husband, murdered in a racist attack which brought up the issue of racism.

Soap operas also show how people deal with these problems so they actually help people get through their problems. For example, someone being racially abused can see how a character on television deals with a similar problem, etc. My class has learned a lot more about moral issues through watching soaps in Religious Studies than we have in our Personal and Social Education lessons. Therefore I agree with the statement.

RELIGION: WEALTH AND POVERTY

a Outline the causes of world poverty. (4 marks)

This would gain full marks because it is a coherent outline of the major causes of world poverty with two described in more detail so that it is not just a list.

Natural disasters are a big cause of world poverty, e.g. floods, hurricanes and earthquakes. Another cause is wars, which can lead to many refugees and cost a lot of money. There are also problems such as: reliance on cash crops, overpopulation, lack of clean water and health care, and lack of education, all of which make it difficult for some countries to move out of poverty. But I think the main cause is debt. The Less Economically Developed Countries (LEDCs) are paying lots of interest to the Western banks. If they could spend this money on development, it would make a big difference.

b Explain how one religious agency is trying to remove the causes of world poverty. (8 marks)

This would gain full marks because it is a comprehensive and coherent explanation which briefly explains how Christan Aid is dealing with eight causes of world poverty. In a question such as this religious specialist vocabulary is not needed.

Christian Aid tries to help after natural disasters by sending emergency supplies to deal with earthquakes, floods and volcanic eruptions. They work with the United Nations to try to bring world peace and they are active in places like Rwanda to bring warring tribes together by creating football leagues. Christian Aid was one of the main founders of Jubilee 2000, the campaign to end Third World debt by persuading banks and governments to cancel debts.

As far as cash crops are concerned, Christian Aid founded Traidcraft which is trying to get a fair price for the products of LEDCs. Christian Aid helps with the lack of education by funding schools in LEDCs, and the problems of inadequate health care by funding clinics and hospitals. Christian Aid has a well-building programme to solve the problem of the lack of clean water and is working on appropriate technology to improve farming methods and reduce desertification so that LEDCs can produce sufficient food.

c 'Only religious organisations can solve world poverty.'
Do you agree? Give reasons for your opinion, by showing you have considered another point of view. (8 marks)

This would gain full marks because it gives an alternative point of view, then it says what is wrong with that point of view in order to come to a personal opinion with a reason. It uses religious reasons and specialist vocabulary (Christianity, Judaism, tithes, pushka, Muslim Aid, Church).

I can see why some people might agree that only religious organisations can solve the problem of world poverty. All religions teach specific things about wealth: Christianity teaches that wealth should be shared with the poor, and Judaism teaches that the tithe should be used (one tenth of income given to the poor) to help the poverty stricken individual get help. The payment of the tithe in Judaism means that from an early age Jewish children are encouraged to put money into the pushka at home for people less fortunate than themselves. Groups such as Christian Aid and Muslim Aid are working to solve world poverty.

However, poverty is not only helped by religious organisations, it is also helped by governments and charities who send aid to places that need it. Organisations such as Oxfam are more often than not non-religious and they provide aid purely for humanitarian reasons. So it is not true that only religious organisations can solve world poverty.

Also, the problems are too vast to be solved by religious organisations. The debt of LEDCs causes many problems through interest payments and these problems can only be solved by banks and governments. Another reason for thinking that religious organisations are not the only ones who can solve world poverty is because of their other attitude to wealth. If, for example, Christians preach that we should share our wealth, why are our churches so ornately decorated? This does not make sense and it is almost as though the Church is being hypocritical. Ornaments and decorations do not mean that it is easier to pray somewhere, they just mean that the church is nicer and more ornate to look at.

So I disagree with this statement and feel that only the governments have enough money to really solve the problem.

The Quality of Written Communication

These answers would gain full marks because:
- they present relevant information in a form that suits their purpose
- the spelling, punctuation and grammar are what would be expected of a grade C GCSE candidate
- They are written in a formal English style using sentences and paragraphs.